Praise for *Human, Nature*

'I love the warmth and refreshing candour of Ian's writing. Readable and relatable – this is an enriching book, from a reliable witness. Highly recommended.'

– Conor Jameson, author and conservationist

'Ian Carter offers highly readable musings on the most pressing issues facing Britain's beleaguered wildlife. Balancing obvious expertise with refreshing honesty ... His infectious passion for the great outdoors sings from every page.'

– Dan Eatherley, author of *Invasive Aliens*

'A deeply engaging account of our complex relationship with the natural world. Drawing on his conservation expertise and lifelong passion for wildlife, Ian explores a wide range of contentious issues and shares the joy of reconnecting with nature in this enlightening, honest and very accessible book.'

– Nic Wilson, nature writer and *Guardian* Country Diarist

'It has been a real pleasure for me as a country-dweller to read Ian Carter's work, because he somehow tells it like it is more than any other rural writer I know ... What he describes is not a fancied landscape cloaked with nostalgia or the ethereal pastures of the far-fetched poet, but a very real place in which birds fly and die in equal measure.'

– Martin Hesp, journalist and novelist

'A wise, thoughtful and very readable series of essays from someone who spent his working life at the forefront of nature conservation, and has now shared his accumulated wisdom with the rest of us.'　　　　－ Stephen Moss, author and naturalist

'A wonderful collection of heartfelt, insightful essays – each one like a privileged chat about the highs, lows and many conundrums of three decades working with nature, from one of its most personable and pragmatic champions. We need people like Ian.'
　　　– Dr Amy-Jane Beer, naturalist, writer and campaigner

'*Human, Nature* deserves to be read very widely … here is a book that considers all the most pressing questions we face as we attempt to understand and fundamentally change our relationship with the natural world. Most importantly, it makes the connections between them, and quietly asserts the need for us to start making more connections – between sites, whole landscapes, and each other.'
　　　　　– Matt Merritt, editor of *Bird Watching* magazine
and author of *A Sky Full of Birds*

Rhythms of Nature

Ian Carter retired early after twenty-five years as an ornithologist with Natural England. He was closely involved with the Red Kite reintroduction programme and wider work on the conservation of birds of prey, bird reintroductions, and wildlife management. The cultural and philosophical aspects of nature conservation have always fascinated him, especially their influence on our attitudes towards the natural world. His recent book *Human, Nature* (Pelagic Publishing 2021) explored some of these relationships and the problems that can arise from them. *Rhythms of Nature* was inspired by four years of living and interacting with wildlife in a sparsely populated corner of Devon, mid-way between Dartmoor and Exmoor.

Rhythms of Nature

Nature

Wildlife and Wild Places
Between the Moors

IAN CARTER

PELAGIC PUBLISHING

First published in 2022 by
Pelagic Publishing
20–22 Wenlock Road
London N1 7GU, UK

www.pelagicpublishing.com

Rhythms of Nature: Wildlife and Wild Places Between the Moors

Copyright © 2022 Ian Carter

A CIP record for this book is available from the British Library

ISBN 978-1-78427-356-9 (Hbk)
ISBN 978-1-78427-357-6 (ePub)
ISBN 978-1-78427-358-3 (ePDF)
ISBN 978-1-78427-402-3 (Audio)

https://doi.org/10.53061/MGSO3829

Cover image: *Swirling Rooks* © Kerrie Ann Gardner

Section-opener images © Richard Allen

MIX
Paper from
responsible sources
FSC® C013056

*To everyone who enjoys straying from the path,
and to my mum and dad for encouraging me to do so.*

CONTENTS

CONNECTIONS

ACKNOWLEDGEMENTS

Time alone in nature is time well spent. But exploring with others leads to shared experiences. Companions may point out things that would have gone unnoticed, or been noticed but left unidentified. And there are the thoughts and ideas that would otherwise not have surfaced, and would certainly not have been discussed. The global pandemic limited travel and resulted in more lone walking than usual while I was writing this book, so the few occasions on which it *was* possible to get outside with others were all the more keenly appreciated. I'm especially grateful to Hazel, Ben, Ali, Margaret, Brian, Jacks, Jon, Danny and Katie for trips in Oxfordshire, Devon and Cornwall; to Gavin and Cliona Dando for visits to their lovely wood and water meadow in Dorset; and to Alick Simmons for wide-ranging discussions about rewilding in a part of Somerset that is helping to show just what can be achieved.

Ali Carter was subjected to the dual horrors of a night walk in the wildest part of Devon we could find within easy reach of the house, and being separated from her phone for several hours (for reasons that will become apparent later).

My uncle and aunt, David and Pam Gibbons deserve a special mention for a kind act that goes back to October 1982. They gave me a copy of the *Reader's Digest Field Guide to the Birds of Britain* for my birthday. That book, more than any other, led to a career in ornithology and a life-long relationship with birds and other wildlife.

My interest in wild foods was enhanced by contributing a weekly piece for Mark Avery's influential blog *Standing up for Nature*, from which some of the writing here has been developed.

I'm grateful to Stephen Todd, who identified the make and model of an old car I found in the woods, based on no more than a smartphone image of a hundred-year-old dashboard posted on Twitter.

Hazel Carter read an early draft of the text and pointed out things that fell flat, as well as points that might work well if only they could be explained more clearly.

The team at Pelagic helped ensure that the route to publication was as smooth and painless as these things possibly can be. Hugh Brazier made insightful comments on the Introduction and the early chapters of the book. David Hawkins edited the whole text, and strayed well beyond the normal bounds of copy-editing when necessary, making good use of his natural history expertise along the way. Nigel Massen was always on hand to answer questions and provide guidance as the project developed. And Rhiannon Robins has made every effort to get the book into as many hands as possible.

Finally, I'd like to thank Natural England, my former employers, for giving me a career in conservation, the chance to visit wild places all over England (and occasionally further afield), and a redundancy package that allowed me to wander around mid-Devon for a while with a reasonably clear head.

INTRODUCTION

Some of my fondest memories are centred on a small, unremarkable pond on the edge of a garden in Oxfordshire. I'm with two young children and we are passing a long-handled fishing net between us, taking turns to sweep it through the water, concentrating on the deeper parts of the pool and the places beneath the thickest weed. Every so often, as the net is lifted up, a slim, writhing creature is revealed. Faces light up, excited cries ring out across lawn, and another Palmate Newt will soon be added to a goldfish bowl resting on a low wall. It surely knows what's coming; it has been caught many times before.

Young children have an inbuilt fascination with nature. They love being outside and can while away hours turning over stones, or dipping a net into water. Apprentice humans are hard-wired to love, and want to learn about, the wildlife all around them. For most of our history, when we lived more intimately with the natural world, this knowledge would have been carried into adulthood and used on a daily basis. These days, children soon lose their love of wildlife amid a swarm of competing interests. Perhaps by the age of ten (or maybe younger), the lure of the screen and the promise of unlimited connection to a wider universe online take over. The newts can rest easy again in their pool, at least until the next generation of young apprentices comes along.

Throughout this book, I'll follow convention in talking about humans as if we are separate from the rest of the natural world, though clearly this is not the case. We represent just one species among many. We have been moulded by the same evolutionary pressures as all other life on Earth. Thinking that we are somehow 'apart' from other creatures is simply a habit we get into – and a rather dangerous one at that – influenced by religion perhaps and by the achievements of modern technology.

There are times when thinking of ourselves as detached from the rest of nature is unavoidable. When I think of protecting 'natural' habitats, humans are, necessarily, outside my thoughts. For instance, I value the surviving areas of pristine forest in the Amazon basin because they have escaped the damaging influence of humans up to now. I view them as 'natural' because humans are *not* part of the picture – at least not in a way that damages the habitat around them. In that sense, a perceived separation between us and everything else *is* meaningful. The American ecologist and philosopher David Abram coined the term 'the more-than-human world', meaning everything in nature excluding humanity.* It's a useful phrase, but a bit of a mouthful for everyday discussions. So, we continue to lean on terms such as 'wildlife' and 'natural' as shorthand when referring to everything on the planet other than ourselves.

There is another reason why it's easy to forget about our past. Although we have been shaped, as have all species, by evolutionary

---

* Abram, D. (1997) *The Spell of the Sensuous: Perception and Language in a More-Than-Human World*. Vintage Books, New York.

forces over immense periods of time, we, and we alone, have broken free from many of the pressures that once ruled our lives. Most of us no longer struggle to find food, or to keep warm and dry. We can treat diseases and injuries that would have finished off our ancestors. In Britain, we have eliminated the predators that once threatened us. And we live in a society where, by and large, we agree not to settle day-to-day disputes through physical force. In that sense, we can indeed be viewed as different from wild animals which still face a daily struggle to survive and reproduce.

It was once suggested to the author Helen Macdonald that 'every writer has a subject that underlies everything they write'.* If that's true, then the common thread running through the chapters that follow is this: all aspects of the ways in which we interact with wildlife and wild places are influenced by our evolved, instinctive responses. The great American naturalist E. O. Wilson put it rather more elegantly: 'having been born into the natural world and evolved there step by step across millions of years, we are bound to the rest of life in our ecology, our physiology, and even our spirit'.† In short, everything we do makes more sense when we think about it in the context of our long evolutionary history.

Though many of us now live largely isolated from the rest of nature, our evolutionary heritage still governs the way we function. I am spooked by large house spiders, even though I know they are harmless. I'm unnerved by walking outside in the dark, though

* Macdonald, H. (2020) *Vesper Flights*. Jonathan Cape, London.
† Wilson, E. O. (1994) *Naturalist*. Allen Lane, London.

I know the local countryside has lost its large predators. I can tune into my hunting and gathering instincts when searching for things to eat in the local countryside. And the same traits are apparent when watching wildlife. My desire to search out new species has, I'm sure, been co-opted from a will to hunt. I'm questing for 'ticks' – to use the birders' jargon – and I relish the pursuit. Others don't bother with that extra step and enjoy hunting for real. The intrinsic thrill of the chase is still there within us, even though we no longer rely on the end product to sustain us.

The way we appreciate the very fabric of the countryside is likely to be governed by predisposition too. Various surveys have suggested that most of us prefer open, lightly wooded, landscapes with water present. Such places provide all that we would once have needed to survive – food, drink, fuel and shelter. We appreciate the open nature of landscapes because we can see a long way and can glean useful information about potential prey and predators from a safe distance. We are less keen on the aesthetics of dense scrub, probably because it obscures sightlines, renders us vulnerable to ambush and makes it more challenging to move around. Water is highly valued because we need to drink regularly, and it attracts other animals that might, in turn, provide us with food. Although these explanations may seem irrelevant to our modern lifestyles, the wiring in our brains is long established and remains with us today; homes beside rivers, lakes and the sea still come at a premium.

A love of visiting and exploring new places is another part of our survival instinct. When we were dependent on wild landscapes, knowledge of as wide an area as possible would have been invaluable. If food dried up, or an influx of predators put us at risk, it would have been important to know where else we could go. For that reason, exploration was useful even if we were settled in a place that, for the moment, offered us all we needed. That urge is still with us today, though modern travel options have vastly extended our reach.

We also have a deep-seated love of the rare and the unusual. A new animal in our garden or local countryside is appreciated more than the common species we see day in, day out. We may admonish ourselves for taking commonplace animals too much for granted, but from an evolutionary perspective it makes perfect sense. There would not have been much point getting worked up about creatures that were ever-present and familiar. But something new would have been worth noticing. It might have indicated a subtle change in the local conditions, an impending seasonal shift or even a new source of food.

Frequently these connections are obvious, if only we pause a while to think about them. They make intuitive sense. Sometimes, though, the way we respond to the natural world is harder to fathom; the connections with our deep past have become hazy and difficult to reconstruct. Almost every March, there will be a day or two when I feel powerfully tuned in to the changing conditions – but I'm not quite sure why, or what to do with the feeling. It's usually around the middle of the month. It's always a day when the wind is light, the sun is out and the temperature has nudged a little higher. The sun feels warm on the skin for the first time in months. It's an odd feeling, broadly pleasurable, but with a strange, melancholy undercurrent and a slightly unnerving sense of urgency about it. It's as if I'm receiving invaluable, privileged information and should be doing something in response – but what?

the woods – has been recognised as beneficial for human health since the 1980s. And in Britain, GPs are now, once again, prescribing time outdoors as a form of treatment, with no negative side-effects and little cost to the nation.

The health benefits claimed for these measures might sound far-fetched; they perhaps bring to mind the dodgy pseudo-science we are familiar with from TV adverts for cosmetics or anti-ageing products. But, in fact, they are supported by comprehensive research. Studies in many countries have confirmed that spending time in nature measurably improves our health and wellbeing. Research is now beginning to establish the mechanisms by which these good things come about.

When we walk in woodland we benefit from the exercise, but we also breathe in volatile chemicals known as phytoncides. These are produced naturally by plants to protect against attack from bacteria, fungi and insects. Some are obvious to us. The powerful aroma of Wild Garlic, for example, is (ironically) caused by a chemical designed to make the leaves less palatable. Mostly we remain oblivious to them. However, when phytoncides enter our bodies, they can boost the number and activity of white blood cells, which help to battle against infection. They may also have a role in preventing certain kinds of cancer. These chemicals are in the air, but the earth too provides us with health benefits. Increasing evidence suggests that microbes present in soil are helpful to us when we ingest them, for both our physical and mental wellbeing.* They are 'old friends' that we have coevolved

---

* The benefits of soil eating and other forms of contact with nature are comprehensively reviewed in Jones, L. (2020) *Losing Eden: Why Our Minds Need the Wild.* Allen Lane, London.

with over millions of years, and they provide us with various essential services once safely inside us. This helps to explain why so many young mammals, including humans, instinctively ingest soil. It perhaps also explains why I once fed soil (and an earthworm) to my baby sister in the back garden. Next time that story is told over a family meal I will have my defence at the ready.

Spending time in nature helps us live lives that are healthier and likely to be longer. We *feel* better after contact with the wildlife around us for one very good reason: we *are* better. If all this sounds too good to be true then we need to remind ourselves of our history and the fact that we have lived in close contact with other animals and plants for millions of years. It would be surprising if, in that time, we hadn't developed intimate, complex relationships – which scientists are only now beginning to unpick. Equally, we should not be shocked to learn that lifestyles increasingly detached from direct contact with nature have adverse consequences for human health.

These days, not many of us retain the strong interest in nature present in childhood through our adult lives. But having taken early retirement a few years ago, I now spend as much of my time wandering the local fields and woods as I did when I was ten years old. I've never truly lost my affinity with the natural world, and so I've eased into this new lifestyle and immediately felt the benefits. I wrote a little of this in my previous book *Human, Nature*. Then, I was in the early stages of adapting to a different life and the book ended on a note of frustration:

Despite our [recent] move to Devon … I spend most of my time indoors, regularly checking in on the wider world through a screen of one sort or another. I remain more detached from close, meaningful contact with nature than I would like. I aspire to do better.

What follows is an account of the progress I've made during the last few years. It is about the various ways I've found to make the most of the wildlife and wild places that remain in the low hills halfway between Exmoor and Dartmoor where we now live. It ranges from the confines of home and garden, out into the local countryside and, finally, to the wildest corners that are still out there but require a little more effort to find. Along the way I have a few suggestions for how to maximise the benefits of time spent outdoors, whether by following a stream (wherever it might take you), picking a route across an unfamiliar, private estate, or heading out into the woods just as the light is beginning to fade.

There is no genuine wilderness left in Britain, it's true, but it *is* still possible to get away from it all and become immersed in the more-than-human world. Despite the competing demands on our time, this is one of the most worthwhile and beneficial things we can do. After all, how many of us ever pause to reflect and think, 'I wish I'd spent more of my time inside the house'?

HOME TURF

HOUSE GUESTS

Whatever the rights and wrongs of thinking we are somehow separate from other life forms, there is one place where we'd like to have things entirely on our own terms. Wildlife tends not to be welcome inside our homes. A nice view of the countryside is fine, and many of us aspire to have gardens rich in wildlife. But in the house, behind closed doors and windows, it's a different matter. We want as few visitors from the non-human world as possible. Of course, we rarely get our way. It is difficult to escape the fact that we're just one of many species, our lives intertwined with those of other creatures around us, even in the sanctuary of our own homes. I'm writing this in mid-September, and downstairs one particular species is reinforcing this point in its hundreds – as it always does at this time of year.

Before we moved to rural mid-Devon, I don't think I'd heard of this creature. Now it provides us with a major source of irritation from August well into the winter, if the weather stays mild. At first, we notice them starting to gather on the white-washed outside walls, mostly on the warm, south-facing side of the house. Then the assault begins. Small numbers gather in the slender gaps between the windows and their frames, secreting themselves out of sight and away from predators, lying in wait until someone swings open the window, when they flop drowsily into the room, and sometimes into your face. It looks very much like a typical House Fly, but this beast is the Cluster Fly, distinguished by a mat of golden hairs on its thorax and its propensity to huddle together with others of its own kind for the winter.*

These window-frame Cluster Flies are a minority. The real swarming masses target the conservatory, finding their way in through a tiny gap where the highest point of the structure is attached to the house. The gap has been plugged perhaps half-a-dozen times, on each occasion with limited success. So they continue to infiltrate, in dribs and drabs, until there are hundreds, even thousands, inside the room. I've just gone downstairs and the count for today (22 September, the autumn equinox) is 524 dead and about 400 alive – determined with as much accuracy as I could muster given that they don't stay still.

In the sunshine, when the conservatory warms up, they buzz incessantly and blunder hopelessly against the windows. The space is all but uninhabitable for humans seeking tranquillity and comfort. But as the sun fades in the evening and the air cools, they become inactive. Only then does the name begin to make sense. They gather in tightly packed groups in the corners of the windows and on the walls, where they will see out the night. This is a clue as to why they enter the house in the first place. They are looking for a secure, cool and sheltered place to overwinter. A loft is perfect, and tens of thousands find their way into ours – to remain there through the coldest months.

---

* The Cluster Fly is a single species *Pollenia rudis*. The superficially similar 'House Fly' is represented by a number of different species that are difficult to tell apart, the most common being the Common House Fly *Musca domestica*.

Those that choose the conservatory find a place subject to extremes of temperature and soon die.

The small numbers that make it into the house have escaped from a whole suite of potential predators outside, but they are far from safe. The main threat comes from irritable humans armed with a vacuum cleaner. We feel guilty for employing such a heavy-handed approach, though reading about their life history helps to assuage this a little: in spring, any survivors will head outside to lay who knows how many eggs in the soil, and the resulting larvae will parasitise earthworms. Meanwhile, there are natural predators on the inside too. The much-feared (by flies and humans) Giant House Spider patrols the floors at night, retreating by day to its sticky traps in undusted corners.* If a fly strays into a web its prospects for seeing out the winter will be greatly reduced.

I'm not a certified arachnophobe but the autumn sorties of this spider across the carpet do make me a little uneasy, especially in the bedroom. I can't kill them, partly out of respect, and partly because of an unshakable fear that the spider community as a whole might seek revenge. So, into a glass and out of the window they go. If you've ever gone to the trouble of taking a spider downstairs to release it at ground level then I can suggest a shortcut. The upstairs windows are fine. House Spiders do not crash to their deaths below when released at altitude. Instead, the legs fan out and they float gracefully down, the right way up, before transitioning nonchalantly between descent and a scuttling dash across the patio.

---

* There are several similar species, but the most widespread has the scientific name *Tegenaria gigantea* so I feel justified in adding 'Giant' to the common name.

I was surprised to learn that House Spiders themselves are vulnerable to becoming spider food. We have lots of spindly Cellar Spiders, or Daddy Long-legs Spiders as they are often called. They are present in most rooms, lurking in corners and along the edges between wall and ceiling, building loose, ramshackle webs and, for the most part it seems, doing precisely nothing. Every so often a female produces an egg sac, out of which hatches a cluster of tiny spiderlings. There may be several dozen in each brood, though all will have dispersed within a few days. I often wonder where they all go.

The adults look unthreatening, with their tiny bodies and long periods of inactivity, but don't be fooled. In our old house I once watched a battle unfold between a Cellar Spider and a House Spider of similar size. The Cellar Spider darted back and forth, throwing a tangle of threads at its rival and quickly immobilising it. Once restrained, it became easy prey. A single bite – and then a prolonged embrace as its insides dissolved and disappeared into the victor.

While my wife, Hazel, has nothing but bad things to say about Cluster Flies and their annual takeover, I can at least point to one significant benefit. As well as providing food for spiders, they are also much sought after by insectivorous birds. In early autumn, the house begins to attract fly-eating species. Wagtails are pre-eminent in the mix. Most common are the familiar Pied Wagtails, strutting across the drive or along the roof tiles, flicking their tails compulsively and every so often launching a darting, mazy attack at a passing fly. Watching them closely reveals why the long tail is so important. In flight, it can be fanned out in an instant, acting as a brake and then a rudder, as a rapid change of direction brings an unsuspecting fly within range.

Less often, we are visited by a lone Grey Wagtail. These are such lovely, elegant birds, with bright lemon-yellow underparts set off against black, white, and subtle powder-grey on the back and head. They are slimmer and more refined than their black-and-white relatives, with an even longer tail. They too loiter around the house, parkouring over the roof and along the window ledges. Once, I managed to sneak up on one that had alighted on the narrow ledge just outside the landing window. Peering through the glass from inside, I needed my reading glasses to focus on it. We watched each other for a few moments – me stock still and holding my breath; the bird living up to its name, pumping its tail while trying to decide whether I was a threat.

We've seen another bird taking advantage of the flies, one that ranks a notch above the Grey Wagtail on two counts. It outscores the wagtail on rarity value. And this particular individual went one better than resting on a ledge just outside the house: it managed to get in. It was late evening. I'd gone to open the back door to let the cat in from our adjoining, open-fronted garage. In pottered our black cat, and at the same time, almost grazing my head, in shot another black creature. It darted straight into the downstairs toilet. I turned on the light and could barely believe that I was looking at a Black Redstart. It must have been roosting in the garage. We'd seen an individual around the house the previous autumn, catching flies on the patio, but to have one inside the house was something rather special. I caught it in my hands as gently as I could and released it back into the garage. By morning it was nowhere to be found.

The Swallows that nest in the garage, and the House Martins under our eaves also take advantage of the abundant insects, skimming just above the guttering, picking off unwary flies. In some years both these birds still have young in the nest into late September, but soon they will all head south, and fuel for the long trip ahead is no doubt very welcome. Even the garden Blue Tits snatch the odd fly while they wait on the gutter of the garage for their turn at the feeders.

I've also seen Hornets try to catch flies around the garden, using a technique that contrasts starkly with the madcap chases of the wagtails and the graceful elegance of the hirundines. The Hornets spot potential prey and smash straight into it, while trying to envelope it in their legs. Perhaps their eyesight is poor, because I sometimes see them doing this to the small tufty flowers that emerge from the Soft Rush stems growing in damper corners of the lawn. They crash into them, testing to see if they are prey before realising their mistake and quickly moving on. The same approach works well enough with flies, though usually only the drowsiest are vulnerable. This may help to explain why Hornets remain active at dusk and even into the night, when the air cools and most insects become far less alert and mobile.

One year, Hornets took over a bat box hung on the telegraph pole at the edge of the garden. This made venturing outside somewhat hazardous. The box was only a couple of metres above the ground, and the worker Hornets transiting to and fro would arrow past on flightlines at about head height. I feared I might swallow one by mistake if my mouth was open at the wrong time. Then, at night, they would try to enter the house, homing in on the windows of lit rooms, tapping menacingly against the panes as if asking to come in. We soon learnt to keep the windows closed after dark, and we would watch as many as six of them together, crawling up and butting against the glass. Just a few millimetres between our protected human domain and everything else beyond.

GROWING THE LAWN

Apart from a hedge alongside the track down to the house, the rest of the habitat in our garden is lawn. Or rather, it's something that could easily become lawn. When we first viewed the property to see if we might rent it from a local dairy farmer, the garden had been neglected for months. There were dense tussocks of grasses and Soft Rush, and brambles were starting to invade, clambering over the low Hornbeam hedge and edging out into the open. The patio was disappearing under a sea of grass, rooted in gaps between the slabs. It was quite a sight, but we signed on the dotted line nonetheless, and the farmer promised he'd 'sort it' for us before we returned. 'Then you can do anything you like with it,' he added, no doubt hoping we'd transform it into a proper cottage garden with an immaculate lawn and flowerbeds. When we returned with our furniture, he'd been true to his word: the whole garden had been crudely flailed to the ground with his tractor. The result wasn't pretty, but at least I'd now be able to start mowing, cutter bar set to the highest level.

I soon got into the familiar mowing routine, more through force of habit than from any desire to live with a perfect lawn. Like many people, I find mowing grass strangely therapeutic, the effect perhaps enhanced because it's a weekly ritual. We often crave peace and quiet when outdoors, so standing behind a badly tuned, raucous petrol engine might not seem a promising way to pass the time. But the brain soon adapts to the noise, and by blocking out other sounds and distractions, the persistent low drone of the engine opens up space to think. Ironically enough, that's when I decided that endless mowing was not the best way forward. An experiment, and a nod towards the new vogue for rewilding, was surely a better option.

The new regime came about partly through laziness, but mostly reflected a genuine desire to encourage more wildlife into the garden. It is quite a large space, but with the lawn cut short there was little structure and, away from the hedge, not much wildlife. Once the grass had been left for a few weeks, that began to change.

To be honest we didn't get quite what we were hoping for. The ill-defined picture in my head was 'wildflower meadow' – and there were a few patches where a meadow-like scene emerged in early summer. We had clumps of Bird's-foot-trefoil, Marsh Thistles, Cow Parsley, Hogweed, and a few Cuckooflowers in the spring in the damper corners. But mostly it was the aggressive and dominant species that took advantage of their new freedom. Dense tussocks of Cock's-foot and other grasses appeared, together with even thicker clumps of Soft Rush. Where there was some bare ground, and I'd hoped wild flowers might get their chance, we were rewarded instead with docks, thistles and impenetrable patches of nettles. Of course, these *are* wild flowers, I told myself repeatedly, just not the ones we had anticipated.

The main problem we faced was one that now affects much of our countryside. It was all down to high nutrient levels in the soil. Nutrients are all-pervasive in modern Britain. They come from slurry added to the fields, from artificial fertiliser and also from the air itself as a result of pollution from farming, industry and road traffic. Despite having mown the grass dozens of times and removed the cuttings (to reduce nutrients), the richness in the soil was still very much there. As can be seen along our local road verges and woodland edges, high nutrient levels favour competitive, fast-growing species that quickly swamp the smaller, less vigorous plants, robbing them of space and light. The result is an abundance of tall grasses, with perhaps some Cow Parsley, Cleavers, Hedge Mustard and Common Nettles, but not much variation, and little chance for the many low, or slow, plants trying to find a way in.

We struggled with the appearance of what we'd created. As a compromise, I decided to mow some winding and – as I imagined them – aesthetically pleasing strips through the longer grass. It helped a little, signalling that the area hadn't been entirely abandoned. But the overall effect of rank vegetation still looked messy. I found, to my surprise, that a mindset influenced by years of indoctrination about tidy, well-kept lawns was hard to shake off. I looked outside and worried what people would think; I worried specifically what my mum and dad would say on their next visit. The farmer, when he came around to reconnect the temperamental water supply, didn't mention anything directly but his eyebrows took a while to return to their normal position. 'I said you could do anything with it, I didn't say do nothing,' he couldn't quite bring himself to say.

The newly 'rewilded' garden may not have worked quite as intended, but already it supported far more plant diversity than a well-managed lawn. We are lucky to have plenty of trees in the area, with an abundance of small woods and hedge-lines. But most of the local fields are intensively managed and support few plants other than the grass itself, perhaps a few rushes and maybe a bit of clover. They are either heavily grazed, resulting in a very short sward and little structure, or regularly cut close to ground level in the summer for silage, sometimes two or three times a year.

Our garden, with its mix of species and varied structure, now stood out from the surrounding fields. We noticed the difference, and it soon became apparent that the local wildlife had spotted it too. The garden was suddenly alive with small mammals. Numerous holes in the thatch of dead grass showed that Field Voles had colonised, and occasionally we'd see one dart for cover as we walked by, dissolving into a tussock and out of harm's way. With the voles came the vole predators – and they finally vanquished any outstanding concerns we may have felt.

I'd already caught sight of a Barn Owl a few times from the window, usually late in the day, beating back and forth over the nearby fields as the light faded. Now when I see one, the routine is markedly different. The owl regularly breaks away from its field patrols and makes a beeline for our garden. Sometimes it sits on the fence to survey the scene for a while. On other occasions it sweeps imperiously across, spending no more than a few seconds above the garden, before moving on. Then there are the heaven-sent visits when it lingers, making a few passes and sometimes pausing in flight, hovering for a second or two before plunging down into the tussocks. So, the house has become a hide, and the local Barn Owls are happy to catch Field Voles a few metres away from it.

We miss the majority of Barn Owl visits. They hunt close to the house mostly after dark, with no more than an occasional eerie screech, heard through a cracked window, to give the game away. But Field Voles get no respite; they risk attack from the air twenty-four hours a day. The day shift is taken up by the Kestrel. This is a scarce bird in the area. I see perhaps one a week on average when out walking, and they are far outnumbered by the local Buzzards. And yet our tiny patch of land now regularly attracts one. It uses the fenceposts and especially the electricity wires as hunting perches – a helpful way to conserve energy in comparison to hovering. Again, we have a ringside view. I watch transfixed as the Kestrel stares down from its perch, head tilting as its interest is piqued. Often, when it spots something, it drops down in stages, with bouts of hovering allowing it to track the prey as it moves stealthily towards it.

We see other vole predators far less often, but they appear now and then to brighten the day. A Fox wanders through the fence every so often in winter, when times are hard and it can't resist the lure of rodents (or chickens) even in daylight. There is the occasional Weasel and Stoat, and once a hooting Tawny Owl gave away its presence on the wires above the lawn; there was still just enough light to make out its plump silhouette. These predators, especially those that hunt by sight rather than sound, must benefit from the short pathways we've cut through the longer vegetation. Small mammals can easily remain hidden and inaccessible in uniform areas of thick grass. But the open strips are more challenging, and they reveal themselves as they pass across. Variety in the structure of vegetation creates opportunities and dangers (depending on your perspective), and almost always helps to support a wider range of different species.

Birds too have benefited from the changes, and this has led us to rethink our attitude towards the dominant plants that we so often deem to be 'weeds'. From late summer through into the winter, the garden in full of seeds. The voles and other small mammals no doubt take advantage, but so too do seed-eating birds. Goldfinches were the first to arrive in pairs and small flocks. On the mown strips they home in on quick-growing dandelions, while in the taller vegetation they head for the thistles. Goldfinches work methodically, but speed is of the essence; they feed on such tiny seeds that many are needed to constitute a decent meal. White fluff drifts away on the breeze, now detached from the seed it is supposed to be dispersing.

Other birds have been more unexpected. The grasses and other plants add so much structure that even birds associated with woodland and hedgerow have become regular visitors. Redpolls occasionally move through the vegetation in autumn. And Bullfinches visit in winter in small, mixed-sex groups, favouring the taller dock and sorrel stems. They bring welcome colour to a drab winter scene, and showcase a contrasting approach to the Goldfinches and Redpolls. A Bullfinch's beak is short and rounded, allowing it to deal with larger buds and fruits rather than delicately picking out small seeds individually. As they shuffle up towards the top of a stem the weight is sometimes too much for the plant, causing the seedhead to arc slowly down to the ground. The birds are clearly used to this happening; they cling on for the ride, casually continuing to feed.

a long, two-handled version with a curved blade at the end for sweeping across, parallel to the ground.

Scything worked well enough, enabling me to deal with the tree seedlings, as well as to remove some of the denser, more dominant clumps of grass and rush, in the hope of encouraging more variety. Voles occasionally darted away as I worked, though they had a high chance of surviving the encounter, unlike the case with mechanical cutting. I also uncovered a few Toads when I inadvertently strayed too close to the ground with the blade. The tussocks made perfect damp, sheltered places for them to hide out during the day, and I wondered if they would hibernate there. Once I'd got into a routine, the work was every bit as therapeutic as mowing, if rather more tiring. And the accompaniment was natural birdsong rather than the artificial drone of an engine.

As with any habitat management, there have been losers as well as winners. In our first winter here, before the lawn experiments, the Redwings and Fieldfares often spilled over into the garden from the adjacent fields, foraging for earthworms. Starlings, Blackbirds, Song Thrushes and Mistle Thrushes were sometimes with them. Meadow Pipits moved back and forth between the wires and the lawn, and that April we had our one and only garden Wheatear, pausing on migration to take advantage of the bare ground where the farmer's flail had scraped away the vegetation.

Now, birds that need access to the ground to forage have less habitat to work with, and have become less common or no longer visit. We are seeing in miniature the dilemma faced by conservation managers across the country. All decisions come with consequences; gains for some species are almost always at the expense of losses for others. Overall though, we're very happy with the results we've seen. And even the farmer seems to be gradually coming around. We've approached the subject tangentially, as is the British way, edging around it by talking about the wildlife we see. He seems genuinely impressed by our tales of Foxes, Barn Owls, Kestrels and Bullfinches feeding close to the house and enriching our lives as we pause to watch them from within.

GARDEN REWILDERS

As a long-term owner of both cats and dogs I'm sometimes asked which of them I'd choose if I could only have one. That's a tough call. Yet there is one animal that, above all others, I wouldn't want to be without. The humble domestic fowl comes with its share of problems and annoyances, but the longer we've kept them, the more highly we've come to value these creatures, both for the direct benefits they bring and for the help they provide with wildlife gardening.

Chickens were a feature of my childhood. We had a small mixed flock of hens and (contrary to the usual advice) several cockerels which were free to roam the garden, often disappearing for hours at a time into neighbouring fields and gardens. My sister and I each got to name our own cockerel. Mine was 'Scruffy', hers 'Hawkeye'. She had the best name but I had the best cockerel. There was the odd mishap with the local Foxes and neighbouring dogs but our small flock remained more or less intact over many years and even came with us when we moved from Cheshire down to Oxfordshire. They appear in old family photos, mostly as casual interlopers in the background, but occasionally held up to the camera with pride.

It took over two decades of adult life before I rekindled the connection. But when we first moved into a house that had a sufficiently large garden, set back far enough from the road, we finally took on a flock of our own. We thought this would be a big undertaking at first, but it was remarkably easy to get started. Our local garden centre stocked point-of-lay hens and we ordered a pre-built mini henhouse. Other than that, all we needed was one sack of corn, one of layers pellets, and wood-shavings for the henhouse. Everything clicked into place with a few minutes of online shopping.

Once installed, the hens almost looked after themselves. Somehow, they knew to roost inside the house. They knew that the boxes on the side were for laying eggs. And they soon learnt that food was easy to find by foraging across the garden. We provided water, threw them the odd handful of corn, shut the door of the henhouse at night, opened it in the morning, and cleaned out the wood-shavings every week. It was no more complicated than that. To prove the point, we were once forced to leave them unattended during our annual two-week holiday when let down by a neighbour at the last minute. We filled up a large pheasant-feeder with grain so they had access to food, and the garden pond provided water. They had to take their chance with the henhouse door being left open, but the garden was securely fenced. When we came back, there they were, casually strolling across the lawn, having barely noticed our absence, and all but indifferent to our return.

The helpful role of hens as garden rewilders dawned on us gradually, by coincidence over roughly the same period as the word 'rewilding' came into regular use. I now think of hens as the miniature garden equivalent of the cattle or ponies used to help manage many nature reserves. Cattle graze the vegetation, keeping down the otherwise dominant grasses so that a wider diversity of wild flowers get a chance. On a much smaller scale, chickens perform a similar role. They keep unmown, wild areas of the garden in check, partly by eating the grass, but mainly with their distinctive approach to foraging. They rake vigorously at the vegetation with their powerful feet to uncover tasty morsels of food – a beetle larva perhaps, or an earthworm if the soil itself is exposed. And they can be encouraged to focus on a particular area though the judicious scattering of corn. This helps reduce the dominance of fast-growing grasses, breaks open the structure of rank vegetation, and creates little patches of bare ground where other plants have a chance to become established.

Where the grass is very thick, the dog sometimes helps out by digging through to the soil below, in her never-ending quest for small mammals. The hens notice the soil flying backwards and move in, hoping to find newly exposed worms or beetles. They have even taken to following the dog around the garden in anticipation that she might start to dig another hole. And they will revisit these spots in the coming days, raking the surface and creating a perfect seedbed for wild flowers.

On a sloping bank in our Devon garden, the thicker grass has gradually been scraped and scratched away. Long-dormant seeds have been brought to the surface and light floods onto the ground. We now enjoy early summer flushes of pink Common Centaury, orangey-red Scarlet Pimpernel and bright yellow Bird's-foot-trefoil, instead of uninspiring uniform grass. The bare patches also provide habitat for invertebrates. Beetles and spiders scuttle across the surface, and solitary bees burrow into it, taking advantage of the warmth of full sunlight.

Is there a downside to hosting hens in a wildlife garden? Well, possibly, though much depends on your philosophy towards wildlife and how flexible and tolerant you are prepared to be. Hens will certainly eat some of the creatures we find desirable as well as those that are more often considered as pests. They are partial to earthworms, but they struggle to access them and therefore don't take very many. They eat small slugs and snails too, which can be seen as a good thing if they are devouring your vegetables, but not so good if you value them as food for garden birds and Hedgehogs.

Some acts of predation are harder to forgive. Hens that find a Frog or Toad become instantly merciless. Fearing they may lose such a large food item to rivals in the flock, they peck away relentlessly, reducing the prey to bite-sized pieces in short order. This is especially frustrating when they come across a Toad, because they don't eat it, presumably because of the distasteful skin. Small mammals suffer a similar fate when their nests are occasionally discovered under the thatch of old dead grass. Even young birds can become victims if they fledge too soon and are ambushed on the ground, a fate that once befell a young Chaffinch as we watched on, helpless, from an upstairs window.

Our response to these incidents has been to improve the habitat in the garden so that our Frogs, Toads and other animals have more places to hide themselves away from patrolling hens. More bushes have been established, and piles of brash and logs have been added to corners. We've found that old railway sleepers are especially favoured by Toads, and we often notice one using the same spot beneath a sleeper for several weeks, resting in safety by day and no doubt emerging to roam the garden at night when the hens (and other predators) pose no threat. Indirectly, then, our chickens have helped to promote further improvement in the garden's wildlife through the mitigation we've provided.

Brown Rats have proved to be an almost constant irritation when we've kept hens. They seem to home in on gardens with chickens, no doubt taking advantage of any surplus food. They've had the audacity to burrow directly underneath our henhouse, throwing out small mounds of black earth all around the edges. Reactions to this species depend on your philosophy. They could be considered a welcome new addition to the garden fauna – but more often they are seen as disease-ridden pests to be eradicated at all costs. I try to nudge myself towards the former view, though if numbers become excessive, or if one Rat manages to find its way into the main house, my resolve is sorely tested.*

Hens have much more to offer than just help with rewilding. There are the eggs, of course, and the pleasure that comes from being able to eat fresh, sustainable produce rather than the factory-farmed equivalents with their disconcerting red stamps. There is also a strange but powerful therapy that comes from having hens in the garden. It's tricky to articulate, and it took us by surprise at first, but there is something remarkably calming about watching hens. There is the slow, methodical foraging as they rake at the ground and peer down hopefully to see if anything

---

* My complex feelings towards the humble Brown Rat are explored in a chapter of an earlier book: see pages 28–32 of Carter, I. (2021) *Human, Nature: A Naturalist's Thoughts on Wildlife and Wild Places*. Pelagic Publishing, Exeter.

edible has been revealed. Sometimes they cover an area as a loose unit, seemingly working together. The pace varies depending on the abundance of food items, slowing down as prey is found, then speeding up again when less productive terrain is encountered – the ultimate expression of concentration and mindfulness, focused solely on the task at hand. Once well fed, they spend their time loafing in a corner, preening their feathers, or settling on a patch of exposed soil to enjoy a dust bath.

As well as being relaxing to watch, there are the restorative benefits of high comedy. A few days ago I watched as two hens locked eyes on the same crane-fly at the same time, before careering chaotically after it, zig-zagging across the ground, propelled by a blur of stunted wings. In the end they were both left frustrated, tilting their gaze wistfully towards the sky as it rose up and away to safety. Grasshoppers on the patio and in the flowerbeds lead to similar pursuits, with frenetic stop–start chases as the prey lands in cover, only to be flushed once again as the attacker homes in.

Adding a cockerel to the mix provides another dimension to flock-watching. They have a distinct air of authority, even arrogance, about them as they oversee their harem. We bought one recently and introduced him to our hens. He was cautious at first but now he struts purposefully around the fringes of the group, keeping an eye on things and, naturally, taking the opportunity to mate when the moment is right, and sometimes when it isn't. But he has a nurturing side too. He indicates the presence of food to the hens by pecking loosely at it and making an endearing, gentle clucking noise – a way of saying that he is happy to forgo it for the sake of the others. He is clearly keen to ensure that the potential mothers of his offspring are kept safe and in good condition.

A cockerel will also maintain vigilance for potential predators, sounding a distinctive low screeching alarm to alert the hens. The local Buzzards regularly elicit a reaction as they pass low overhead. Rarely, a Buzzard will land on the edge of our roof, where it is watched warily by the cockerel, head tilted to the horizontal so that one eye can be kept fixed on the intruder above. He went one better the other day by finding a Red Kite for me. The screeching call drew my attention as I was weeding the patio. The hens froze and as I looked up, there it was, circling low over the garden, one of just a handful that I've seen here in mid-Devon.

Based on the evidence of the last few weeks, a cockerel can also help to keep stray Pheasants away from the garden. In previous winters they have arrived in numbers after the start of the shooting season, eating the hen food and jumping up onto the bird table, clearing it within seconds. Only the other day, I saw the cockerel vigorously chase a cock Pheasant away from the hen feeder – and it has yet to return. So far, the anticipated mass arrival of hen Pheasants has been held at bay. They wander about in the adjoining fields but seem reluctant to come through the fence.

The frequent bouts of territorial crowing are a real pleasure or a major source of irritation, depending on your mindset. Most chicken keepers hold it up as one of the finest and most evocative sounds of our countryside, but near neighbours will not necessarily agree. After loud music, yapping dogs and compulsive DIY, crowing cockerels are probably next on the list for neighbour disputes about noise. Thankfully, we live far enough away from our neighbours that this is not a problem.

Hen therapy comes with a health warning, however. If you're going to keep chickens, a certain amount of stoicism and tolerance is called for. We have lost part, or all, of our flock to the local Foxes on several occasions. Sometimes carelessness has cost us. A gap in the garden fence unplugged for one day too long, or a henhouse door inadvertently left open overnight. On other occasions there was nothing much we could have done. The garden of our current house is impossible to fence securely. One morning last year, I looked out of the window to find my gaze met by a Fox. It lifted its head to stare back at me from the far edge of the drive. It was panting vigorously and had, a moment before, been eyeing up a lone white hen. I went out to chase it away and began to piece together what must have happened. Our flock of four (already two down from its peak) was now a flock of one. Trails of bloodied feathers led away into an adjacent field. The panting now made sense. The Fox was out of breath because it had just killed, carried away and then stashed the other three birds before coming back for a final time. The result was even more dispiriting than a total absence of hens: a single, sorry survivor, clucking forlornly, witness to unspeakable events and no doubt fearing that worse was to come.

A few months after we had restocked, we returned from a walk to find a worrying puff of white feathers on the lawn and an apparent absence of hens. The signs were ominous. After a search of the garden, we tracked two of them down to the henhouse, hunched miserably on a perch towards the back. At least there were survivors. A few minutes later we found the rest of the flock, tucked away under cover of the thick hedge that flanks the drive, and requiring a lot of persuasion to come out. We put it down to a lucky escape from a Fox attack, and kept a wary eye out the following day. It was then, as I was scanning the garden and nearby field for Foxes that I noticed a Buzzard overhead – high at first but dropping lower and turning in ever tighter circles as it drifted closer to the house. The hens saw it too, and rather than keeping a wary eye on it, which is their typical response, they ran for the hedge in panic. It must, I'm sure, have been a Buzzard that attacked them the previous day, the stray feathers on the grass suggesting it had come close to making a kill.

It would be easy to become frustrated by these events, especially if your children have lovingly named their favourite hen. But I try to see such things as an essential part of living in a landscape that is still rich enough to support wild animals, even those that can occasionally cause problems. I'm happy to accept that the Fox has young to feed and a rightful place in our countryside. Away from the garden, it's an animal I love to see. We always pause before each restocking, fearing that the same thing will happen again. But, after a short gap, we submit to the inevitable. I wouldn't want to live for long without a band of garden hens, for their help with the gardening, the calming atmosphere they bring and (stoicism to the fore) the way they help reconnect us to the wider landscape.

Postscript

Ironically enough, the greatest gift from our latest batch of hens came after they were gone. Following a long period without a

Fox sighting, the old problem resurfaced. Once again, we acquired a resident Fox close to the garden, probably a young animal born in the spring trying to find its way in the world. And it had struck gold. Our twelve-strong flock of hens was too great a temptation, and individuals were being picked off one by one. The long grass of the rewilded lawn offered thick cover so the hunter could slip unseen to within striking range. The cockerel did his best, calling frantically (once, memorably, intruding on a podcast) and charging towards danger when a hen had been caught, but he was as powerless as we were. Before long we were down to six hens and felt obliged to pen the survivors out of harm's way. For a few days we watched as they paced miserably up and down their new boundary trying to fathom a way out, and then we relented and gave them to a neighbour. She had the space (and a regime of Fox control) to allow them to roam safely.

A few weeks later in mid-September I glanced out of the window and a blob on top of one of the fenceposts caught my eye. As any birder will tell you, some blobs seen at a distance invite close scrutiny, for reasons that defy logical explanation; intuitively, I felt this might be something good. I grabbed the binoculars from the kitchen and pulled the fencepost into sharp focus. Such was my shock that it took a full minute or so for a bird that is impossible to misidentify to resolve itself into... yes there could be no doubt... into a Wryneck. It sat there on its post for a while and then flopped down into the grass and out of sight.

Over the next few days I watched it regularly, sometimes on the fence but more often foraging along the bank nearby at the edge of the drive. This was an area much favoured by the hens

been Common Pipistrelles. Bizarrely, we once found one at the bottom of a plastic bucket in the garage early one morning. How it ended up there is anyone's guess. We also encountered a Brown Long-eared Bat resting in the corner of the garage one evening and guessed that it too would be making use of the hedge when foraging for moths, beetles and other large insects.

When we first moved in, I put up three wooden Dormouse boxes, attaching them to Hazel stems, tucked away within the hedge. They have not yet attracted the target species – but Blue Tits have used them for nesting, despite the hole facing inwards towards the tree, and another delightful mammal often reveals itself when I peek inside. Wood Mice stuff the boxes with dry leaves as bedding and lay in stores of Hazel nuts in case food becomes hard to find. They are agile animals, lightning fast, and sometimes leap clear of the box as I gently lift the lid. It's difficult to be too disappointed, but one day I hope to find its rather less jumpy relative, perhaps an individual drawn in by the new shoots of life and the thicker cover. If that happens then my amateurish attempts at hedgerow management will have added something of great value to this place.

TO FEED OR NOT TO FEED

I'm increasingly conflicted on the subject of feeding garden birds. On the one hand, these are wild creatures and I'm reluctant to interfere with their natural behaviour. On the other, feeding helps keep them alive through the challenging winter months. And, thinking of myself rather than the birds, I enjoy watching them at close range, near to the house. Despite reservations, I put food out most days from September through to March or April.

Our feeders hang from the old hedge that runs along the track to our house and ends just across the drive from the kitchen window. They help make the chore of washing-up a little less tedious. I'd find it difficult to stop, but often, when I'm cleaning the dishes, I fret about the consequences beyond keeping a few more birds alive over winter. What are the effects of this meddling on the local bird populations? And what might those effects look like at a bigger scale given that so many of us now provide food for birds?

I'm probably a little old-fashioned in the foods I put out. Mixed seed, peanuts, sunflower seeds and fat balls are about as adventurous as it gets. I did once try the tiny, jet-black nyjer seeds, having read that they are favoured by Goldfinches. The experiment failed, though Goldfinches are now regular visitors and seem perfectly happy with sunflower hearts; score one for the traditional approach. I've yet to be tempted by mealworms or waxworms, though they apparently attract a wider range of birds, including insect eaters such as Wrens, Pied Wagtails and even Treecreepers.

When the bird-feeders go back up it feels like an admission that summer is drawing to a close once again. The birds are slow to cotton on at first, and natural food is usually plentiful at this time. But as the temperature starts to fall, word gets around and numbers begin to build up. I guess that survivors from the previous winter check the site regularly, knowing that it has been productive in the past. And when they resume their routine of regular visits, the young of the year follow their lead.

In cold weather, especially later in the winter when natural food is scarce, the number of birds using the feeders is impressive. Most abundant is the Blue Tit. My best count so far is seventeen, all either on the feeders or waiting their turn in the hedge close by. With help from the less common species they work their way through perhaps five fat balls and a long feeder of peanuts *every day*. How many individual Blue Tits visit during a typical winter is anyone's guess, but given the constant toing and froing along the hedge-line I suspect it might creep into three figures. I'd love to know.

While the Blue Tits are a near-constant presence, it's all or nothing with the Long-tailed Tits. In winter these birds travel in small flocks, up to about fifteen strong. Each group has its own patch and moves around it in wide circuits to help improve foraging efficiency. They feed for the most part on invertebrates, which react to disturbance from foraging birds by flying away, by staying still and relying on camouflage, or by retreating into cracks and crevices. This reduces the hit rate for birds, and means that it's best for them to keep moving into areas that have been free of disturbance for longer, where prey is more likely to be caught off guard.

I happened to be watching my parents' bird table one day as the regular Long-tailed Tit flock arrived. As was their habit, they headed across to this reliable food source from the nearby cherry tree. Only, today, it wasn't reliable. In fact, it was missing entirely. My dad had taken the table into the garage to add another feeder. The birds, in twos and threes, took it in turns to fly out to the exact spot where it had stood, hovering there for a few seconds as if disbelieving their own eyes, before returning to the cherry tree.

Artificial feeding has some obvious impacts on birdlife as well as a few that are trickier to pin down. Most noticeable is the way that feeders concentrate local birds into small areas. I see this in and around our garden, and I experienced a more striking example a few years ago at the RSPB's headquarters at The Lodge, Sandy. I had a spare half-hour before a meeting and decided to walk around the nature reserve, a wonderful mix of woodland and restored heathland. The reserve looked fantastic but there was something missing: there were hardly any birds. When I got back to my car I understood why. On the far side of the car park was an impressive array of well-stocked feeders, buzzing with activity. All the typical species were represented: Chaffinches, Greenfinches, the common tits, Nuthatches, as well as dozens of Siskins and Redpolls, and several handsome Bramblings. On the ground there were Blackbirds, Robins and Dunnocks, picking up scraps that had fallen from above. All the woodland birds were here, in the car park. Instead of gleaning fruits, berries, seeds and invertebrates from the nature reserve, they were gorging on food shipped in specially for them from distant parts of the planet.

It's clear, then, that feeding changes patterns of behaviour. But what about changes to the balance and make-up of wild bird communities? Here is a plausible scenario, albeit one that is difficult to prove: Great Spotted Woodpeckers come regularly to most feeding stations. They are bigger than the finches and tits and have a powerful bill that smaller birds do well to keep away from. They can push their way to the front of the feeding queue whenever they fancy, and feed for as long as they want.

Great-spots have increased in recent years. The population has more than quadrupled since the late 1960s. They have colonised new areas, especially in northern England and Scotland, and have also made the leap across the sea to Ireland. It is almost certainly true that garden feeding has aided this process. Surely this is a good thing, worth celebrating? Well, it's certainly good for the Great Spotted Woodpecker. But what about the species with which it competes for food and nest sites come the breeding season? And what about the species that *are* food? While the woodpecker's diet is dominated by invertebrates, it will also take nestlings, and to get to them it will break into nests in tree holes and nest boxes. There is no proof, but competition and predation by Great-spots has been suggested as a possible contributory factor in the decline of the Marsh Tit, Willow Tit and the now perilously rare Lesser Spotted Woodpecker, among other species.

Here is another possibility. Burgeoning populations of resident Blue Tits and Great Tits, propped up by bird food, have probably increased the competition for nest sites with other hole nesters. As well as Marsh Tits and Willow Tits, hole-nesting Pied Flycatchers have also declined over recent decades. Willow Tits have gone completely in our area, and Pied Flycatchers are now very scarce. Marsh Tits are far less abundant than they once were, and I only ever see a single pair at the feeders. A direct effect is hard to prove, but it is believed that increased competition for nest sites from Blue Tits and Great Tits has made life far more challenging for other hole-nesting birds.[*]

The consequences of feeding at a national scale are difficult to study, but research is finally starting to reveal some of them. Around half of all households in Britain put out an estimated 60,000 tonnes of food each year (at a cost of £300 million), enough to sustain a remarkable 196 million birds.[†] Wild bird communities are, indeed, being reshaped as a result. Birds that readily take advantage of this food, including Blue Tits, Great Tits, Goldfinches, Siskins and even Woodpigeons, have done well, with numbers rising sharply in recent years – including in built-up areas where feeding in gardens is common. Certain red-list species, including Starlings and House Sparrows, have

---

[*] The following review paper provides an excellent overview of the likely effects of food provisioning on birds in Britain: Lees, A. C. and Shutt, D. (2021) Killing with kindness: Does widespread generalised provisioning of wildlife help or hinder biodiversity conservation efforts? *Biological Conservation* 261: https://doi.org/10.1016/j.biocon.2021.109295

[†] Plummer, K. E. *et al.* (2019) The composition of British bird communities is associated with long-term garden bird feeding. *Nature Communications* 10: https://doi.org/10.1038/s41467-019-10111-5

declined but numbers would no doubt have fallen more steeply in the absence of feeding. Birds that do not visit feeders regularly are less likely to have increased, and some have declined sharply.

It's worth keeping in mind that species interact with each other in ways that are sometimes obvious but more often are complex and challenging to disentangle. One possibility is that resident woodland birds gain an advantage over migrants. In the past, severe winters would have knocked numbers back every so often, reducing competition with returning migrants in the spring. Now, our residents are sustained at artificially high levels with limitless food. When the migrants return, they may struggle to find vacant nesting territories. Pity the poor Pied Flycatcher returning from Africa to a wood chock-full of Blue Tits and Great Tits, desperately seeking a free hole in which to nest. Whenever there are winners, it is a near certainty that there will also be losers.

Another issue of concern is disease. Many of them spread more easily if birds are concentrated in small areas, and busy feeding stations provide an obvious focal point. One disease, trichomonosis, is thought to be responsible for the loss of over two-thirds of Britain's Greenfinches in just ten years – a stark illustration of the damage that can be done.* In recent years, Chaffinches have shown a sharp drop in numbers, and disease is high on the list of likely causes. Other species too can be affected, with sick Great Tits, House Sparrows, Woodpigeons and Collared Doves often reported from gardens. We hear much

---

* Lawson, B. *et al.* (2012) The emergence and spread of finch trichomonosis in the British Isles. *Philosophical Transactions of the Royal Society B*: https://doi.org/10.1098/rstb.2012.0130

about the need for regular cleaning of feeders, and we are advised that sites should be changed regularly to try to reduce the risk. Yet the dangers in encouraging such close proximity are impossible to eliminate entirely.

Even bird food itself can cause problems. Various toxins are produced by the moulds that are regularly found on peanuts and in seed mixes when they are tested. This is another area where more research would be helpful to determine the extent and scale of the problem.

So, feeding birds alters their natural behaviour. It concentrates them in small areas and it restructures the balance of local bird communities. Further, through competition or disease, it can cause individual species to decline, sometimes dramatically. It also relies on setting aside land in the tropics and subtropics to grow peanuts and other foods, and so contributes to climate change. Then there is the environmental cost associated with transport. It is big business but is it really sustainable in a climate and biodiversity emergency?

Set against that, feeding can improve survival rates for certain species and brings pleasure to millions of people. It also contributes to the coffers of wildlife charities, as well as to the wider economy.

There is plenty to think about every time I stand at the sink, looking out to the hedge and the feeders that hang from it. Will I beat my count of seventeen Blue Tits? Will I ever see more than two Marsh Tits together? And will the local woodland ever regain its Pied Flycatchers? If I'm honest, I struggle to justify feeding based on logical arguments about the way birds respond to it and the wider ecological and environmental impacts. This

of the seasons. Everything else continues to rely on this funda-
mental celestial measure.

After the shortest day, birds are far more willing to offer up
snatches of song, especially when the weather is settled. Even in
late December they have started to anticipate the coming spring
and I begin to hear hesitant notes from around the garden. It's
all a little half-hearted at first, but come the spring equinox in
March most of our resident songbirds will be singing loudly and
persistently, and some will already be building their nests. By the
time of the longest day, in late June, breeding will be well underway
or even finished for another year. From then on, song drains slowly
from our landscapes once again, as the nights begin to lengthen.

The night sky offers another link to things that are outside our
control and beyond full understanding, as well as a way of tracking
the seasons. Many of the stars visible in the sky change predictably
through the year; I'm familiar only with a few of the most
prominent constellations but for me they have come to stand for
the seasons they preside over. In the northern hemisphere, Orion
looms large through the coldest months of winter, the brightest
of its stars already visible by the end of the afternoon. The three
bright stars that make up the summer triangle (from three
different constellations Aquila, Cygnus and Lyra) hang high
overhead through the warm summer months, though they remain
invisible until darkness falls in late evening. In contrast, looking
to the north, the same constellations are present all year round.
The faint North Star stays resolutely in the same spot because

it lies due north, on the axis around which the Earth spins. The familiar saucepan shape of the Plough (or Great Bear), which points to the North Star, will always be somewhere close by – a comforting and familiar touchstone throughout the year.

I see in these seasonal patterns, parallels with our common, widespread birds. Orion is prominent during the coldest months, when Redwings and Fieldfares are spilling from the hedgerows into the local fields. The summer triangle is overhead on warm nights when the Swallows and House Martins are waiting patiently at their nests or roosts for daylight to return. Or it provides a backdrop to a late-night trip to see Nightjars or to hear the ethereal song of the Nightingale. It becomes more difficult to see in the autumn, much like the Swallows, as it falls lower in the sky. And then, like the Swallows, it disappears completely for the coldest months. As with our summer migrants, we must wait until spring for it to return. In contrast, the Plough and its close associates represent our common residents. Like the Blackbird, Wren, Dunnock, Robin and Chaffinch, they are there with us through all four seasons, through good times and bad.

I sometimes look up at the night sky and try to picture our ancestors doing the same thing. It feels like a connecting thread back to ancient times. And yet the shapes of our familiar constellations are constantly changing. On the scale of a human lifetime, the patterns remain true, as does the timing of their appearance in the sky through the seasons. But, in reality, the stars involved are all hurtling through space in every direction, and at wildly different speeds. So, actually, our distant ancestors would have looked up into a night sky with none of the same patterns that we take so much for granted.

It's not just their relative positions in the sky that are subject to change, but the very existence of the stars themselves. We see stars not as they are but as they once were; their light takes a truly cosmic amount of time to reach us. The vast distances involved lead to some unsettling conclusions. Most of the starlight that enters our eyes began its journey before we were born. Take the three prominent stars that make up Orion's belt: if they had all ceased to exist in 1000 BCE then we would notice nothing until two of them flickered out of sight around 200 years from now. The third would finally vanish from view sometime around the year 3000. We have no way of distinguishing them, but some of the stars are already ghosts.

The planets are more haphazard than the constellations in their appearances. No regular patterns are discernible to the untrained eye. These days, of course, there are apps to tell us exactly what we are looking at. But a little inbuilt knowledge adds to the experience. The brightest planets – Jupiter, Venus, Saturn and Mars – are often more brilliant than any visible star. They don't make their own light but shine only because their surface reflects the sun, and they have a firm, steady light. The stars are distant balls of blazing gas, like our own sun, but *much* farther away, and the brightest ones can be seen to flicker (or twinkle) because of the huge distance the light has to travel and the way it is refracted before it reaches us. With a little practice, this knowledge alone can be used to distinguish between a bright star and a planet.

But which planet? That's trickier, though there are some distinguishing features. Mars glows an eery red, betraying the nature of its rocks. Saturn has its rings, which can be made out with good binoculars (just), or more clearly through a birdwatching telescope. And Jupiter has moons. There are dozens of them, but four can usually be seen through binoculars, showing as tiny prickles of light, strung out in a line each side of their giant host. Venus is often referred to as the morning or evening star. It orbits nearer to the sun than Earth and so is always close to the sun in the sky. In daylight, it can't be seen, but just after sunset (in the west) and just before dawn (in the east) it may give itself up for a few hours. It's closeness to Earth and highly reflective surface explain why it is the brightest of all the planets.

Our own moon has a special draw and power, both real and imagined. It pulls the oceans around and it plays with our minds if we let it. My parents remind me that I'd sometimes refuse to go to sleep as a child until I'd tried to see the moon and either succeeded, or satisfied myself that it was hidden by cloud or not present in the sky that night. This pock-marked sphere of rock circles us every month, following its own routine and offering another way in which we can keep track of timelines here on Earth. From a delicate, thin crescent it increases a little in size each night as it waxes, until it shines out as a full moon, roughly once each month. Then it wanes, back to a slim crescent before disappearing completely, only to return a few days later as the cycle begins once more.

As with the planets, we see the moon only because the sun's light is reflected from its surface. When it is on the far side of the Earth to the sun, the whole surface receives light and is visible to us. But when it moves around so that it is almost between us and the sun, the light catches the edge and we see only the thinnest of slithers.

The darker areas of the moon are known as seas because that's what they were mistaken for by early astronomers. Actually, they are areas where volcanic activity has produced rocks that are less reflective than the rest of the surface. The moon is a stunning object when viewed with binoculars, or even better through a birding telescope, especially in its crescent form when the texture of the seas and craters stand out most clearly.

The moon always looks bigger when low down in the sky than when riding high overhead. This so-called moon illusion is a trick of perspective, resulting from proximity to the horizon. The illusion is so powerful that many people refuse to believe that the size difference is not real. But it's easy to confirm by matching the moon's size to one of your fingernails held out at arm's length. It will take up the same amount of space wherever it is in the sky.

Dust in the atmosphere gives the moon an ethereal yellow or orange glow when it's low in the sky. This is exacerbated in the autumn by dust from harvesting crops and in September or October (depending on the year) the harvest moon is well known for this. The full moon always rises in the east just as the sun is setting in the west. In summer this means that it appears late in the evening when most of us are indoors. But by the autumn it has become an earlier event.

The moon is a constant, reassuring presence through our lives. When I think back to 'Eastfield', the old family home where I grew up, there is one memory that stands out above all others

– the view from my old bedroom on perhaps a handful of evenings each year. I can see it now: stark, leafless winter trees where the woods meet the back lawn, and a huge, butter-coloured moon rising up behind skeletal branches as darkness settles over the garden. I can remember sitting back in bed, head fixed in position, so that I could make out the moon's slow but relentless movement against the horizontal branch of a Beech tree, watching as it touched the bottom edge, and not allowing myself to move until it had started to emerge into the blackness above the same branch. I still do the same thing occasionally, today, using the edge of a window frame. It takes me straight back to that old, familiar house.

By staggering coincidence, the moon is 400 times smaller than the sun but 400 times closer to Earth. As a result, they both take up exactly the same amount of space in the sky, something that occasionally results in a total solar eclipse, the moon slipping perfectly over the disc of the sun. Another seemingly remarkable coincidence is that the moon spins at precisely the rate required to keep the same face presented towards Earth as it orbits – hence the unseen and (until recently) unknowable dark side. Evidence for divine intervention? Perhaps not, but, once again, it plays with your mind.

Ancient humans would have followed the moon's progress with interest as a valued illuminator of the night to aid hunting, to avoid predators and, in more recent times, to help gather in the crops. They would no doubt have been aware that a full moon casts far more than twice as much light as a half-moon: it is around ten times as effective as a light source. This is because the moon is directly opposite the sun when full, and so light hits it straight on from the Earth's perspective, with more of it reflected to us. In contrast, the landscape of the illuminated part of a crescent or half-moon is partly in shadow, making it more interesting to look at with a telescope but far less effective at lighting up the Earth.

Just after the full and new moons, when the Earth, moon and sun are lined up, the gravitational pull from moon and sun work together. At these times, the sea reaches higher up the beach and falls further back, revealing more of the lower shore. Early humans, eyeing the shoreline for a spot of foraging, would surely have considered the state of the moon to plan the timing of their visit.

We have no need to track the moon's progress so carefully these days. I often notice it and have no idea where it is in its cycle. Luckily, there's a handy trick. In the northern hemisphere, if it can be made into an imaginary (lowercase) 'b' by adding a stem then it is '<u>b</u>eginning' and will get <u>b</u>igger each night until full. If the addition of a stem turns it into a 'd' then it is in <u>d</u>ecline and will <u>d</u>ecrease a little each night.

The Earth shines when it is bathed in sunlight, much like the moon. This is obvious in photos taken from space, but it is also revealed by the moon itself in certain conditions. The familiar sight of a slim, bright crescent with the rest of the moon's surface faintly visible is sometimes referred to as 'the old moon in the new moon's arms'. It happens because sunlight falling on Earth shines back out into space and is caught by the moon, including the areas not lit directly by the sun. Just as light from a full moon illuminates our fields at night, so the sunlight reflected from Earth is enough to shine upon the moon's seas and craters – and then back again to our earthbound eyes.

One thing about our night sky is changing rapidly. It is no longer a wholly natural refuge if you are seeking solace and distraction from modern life. Ever greater numbers of satellites are being launched, and many of them are visible as they trace across the sky, taking a minute or two to pass over. I'll never forget seeing my first, about thirty-five years ago on a late-night walk back to my university accommodation. I was dumbfounded that a human-made object, out there in space, beyond the boundaries of our atmosphere, could be seen from the ground. These days it's all too easy to see four or five within a few minutes, and some, including the International Space Station, are brighter than the brightest stars or planets.

All the distant bodies we see out there in the night seem impossibly remote, unknowable and otherworldly. And yet we have the understanding, and the mathematics, to be able to predict the timing and location of their passage across the sky with astonishing accuracy. Does that lessen the magic just a little? If so, then it might explain why the objects I most delight in seeing are still well beyond the reach of human predictions. The timing of meteor showers is known well enough, and the same ones come around at the same time each year. But the appearance of each individual meteor, its brightness, and the direction it will take across the sky are all down to chance. For once, an app won't help.

Meteor showers are named after the constellation from which they appear to radiate. We have the Orionids, Perseids, Leonids and Geminids, to name four of the best known. And each produces shooting stars that have subtly different characteristics. As well as the number of meteors per hour, the colour and brightness vary, as do the speed at which they streak across the sky and the likelihood that they will leave a trail behind them. If you're a fan of slow-moving yellow fireballs then try the Alpha Capricornids in late July, though don't expect to see very many. Two weeks later come the far more abundant Perseids, which tend to be bright and fast, and sometimes leave a trail.

Every meteor I see is a small, unexpected, but wonderful shock to the system; a flash and a trail across the blackness, gone before there is time to pause and dwell on the spectacle. A scrap of rock that has existed, in some form, somewhere, for countless millennia, enters our atmosphere and, in a last blaze of light and speed, is gone.

There is one final, time-honoured, way of appreciating how the Earth moves in relation to the rest of the universe: its daily spin on its own axis. It's easy to forget that we are all hurtling through space at upwards of 1,000 kilometres per hour.* Watching a sunset (or sunrise) is one way we can get some sense of that speed. Only at these times does the sun's proximity to the horizon allow the pace of movement to be seen clearly. Any low, reasonably level, horizon will work but the sea is by far the best place. It is completely flat, and the play of light across the water adds to the magic. Once the bottom of the sun touches the horizon, it

---

* The speed varies with latitude and is effectively zero at the poles because they sit at each end of the axis around which the Earth spins. For the same reason, at the poles, the sun (when it is visible) stays fixed at roughly the same height in the sky through each day.

begins to sink at such a rate that the turning globe becomes a believable reality. Just a few seconds later and it will be gone completely for another day.

If your luck is in, you might even see the fabled 'green flash' in the last moment before the tip of the sun finally slips away. This is caused by the way that light is refracted and scattered in the atmosphere, and it is best seen on a day when the air is clear and stable. I've seen it just twice in fifty years. The last time was a few years ago on a family holiday near Tintagel in north Cornwall. Seven of us were stood on the high cliffs looking out over the sea and witnessed a climax to the day so stunning that we felt like applauding – a final brief pulse of green light, and then nothing but the gradual dimming of the sky towards nightfall.

VENTURING OUT

SIGNS OF LIFE

Many of our best-loved animals can be tricky to observe in the flesh. Mammals are often most active after dark, and although some have managed to adapt to urban life, those in rural areas tend to keep their distance from humans, for good reasons. We are aware of them mainly through seeing their shattered bodies on the side of the road, or from the signs they leave behind.

Badgers are a case in point. They are surprisingly common across much of the country but, unless you make a special effort, it's easy to go years at a time without seeing a live one. Some people have never seen a living Badger, or at best have glimpsed one in the car headlights as it shuffles across the road late at night. They have their distinctive setts of course; there can be few country dwellers who have never stumbled across one when out walking. And because they stick to familiar, well-used routes when travelling from place to place, they also leave evidence of their movements.

With practice, Badger paths are easy to find, showing as narrow strips of flattened soil or vegetation, connecting their setts and the places they go to find food. In our local fields these paths are suddenly revealed in spectacular detail when the grass is cut for silage. As the grass in a field grows up, the leaves close to the ground become faded and yellow, due to a lack of light – an effect that is all too obvious if you cut your lawn after a few weeks of letting it grow. But along the Badger paths, the grass has been trodden down and sunlight floods in, allowing new leaves to flourish. Then, when the field is cut, these paths show as a network of dark green lines, winding across a pale-yellow backdrop. It's pleasing to be able to see the routes they take – brockways if you will – with such clarity, though in an area dominated by dairy farming, advertising presence in this way is not necessarily a good idea; a programme of Badger culling is currently in progress to try to reduce tuberculosis outbreaks in cattle. I wonder how many farmers have noticed these trails and followed them into the surrounding woodlands where the Badgers hide their setts.

In woods much visited by people it's sometimes difficult to distinguish between human and animal pathways, but follow a path for long enough and all becomes clear. A Badger or Fox will pass underneath fallen trees and branches if there is space, whereas people are forced to go around or over the top. The same is true for fence lines at the edge of the wood, and here barbed wire brings an added bonus: tufts of hair can be found snagged on the lower strand, revealing the animal that passed through. Badger hairs are particularly distinctive, being stiff and wiry, with alternating bands of black and white. They may be more familiar to half the population through their use in shaving brushes – mostly synthetic these days, though the real thing is apparently still imported from China.

Animals leave tell-tale prints as another giveaway of their presence. Suitable muddy surfaces tend to be few and far between, so the evidence is patchy and hard to find. But snow changes everything. It primes the landscape in brilliant white, providing a surface that reveals every movement. After a good snowfall I tend to walk the fields closest to home, relishing the chance to learn more about animals that come by after dark but usually pass through unnoticed. After snow, they are caught in the act. By following their trails, I can find out where they have come from, whether or not they entered the garden and, if so, which direction they went next. For a wild animal, rural gardens are just another part of the territory rather than being in any way separate from the rest of the countryside.

Following a trail in snow offers much more information than can easily be gleaned from watching the animal itself. Even if you have night vision equipment, keeping in close contact with a Fox or Badger for any length of time is almost impossible. Sooner or later it will become aware of your presence and slip quietly away, or cease to behave naturally. Snow provides an uninterrupted picture of hours of activity if you are willing to follow the signs and piece together the story.

Fox trails are especially good fun to trace because this is such an adaptable and flexible creature; a trail could lead almost anywhere. They also leave plenty of clues along the route as to what they have been up to. A typical feature in grassland is an abrupt end to the line of footprints, a gap of two feet or so of pure, untouched snow, and then an explosion of powder with a hole in the middle. This is a Fox pausing, having picked up the sound of a small mammal moving about beneath the snow. It has then leapt forward with all four paws (and muzzle) landing in the same spot, punching a hole through to its potential meal.

If there are spots of bright red sullying the snow, then you'll know it was successful.

Badgers leave highly distinctive prints with four or five large pads aligned in a shallow semi-circle. I've yet to find any inside our garden but the snow has shown that they visit the adjacent fields, and have walked by just the other side of the fence.

Camera traps now offer a simple and reliable way of revealing nocturnal visitors to gardens, but they lack the magic of tracking and at best provide a snapshot rather than the whole story. They are no substitute for a few hours of detective work.

The mammal that is most evident in this part of Devon, both in the flesh and from the signs it leaves behind, is the Red Deer. This is Britain's largest land mammal and it moves around the local fields and woods in groups of thirty or more. The large, rounded droppings are very obvious and I sometimes find patches of flattened grass or Bracken where they have clearly been resting. A cast antler is a rare (and highly coveted) find, but small trees with the bark stripped are a common sight, especially after the rut; the testosterone-fuelled stags show off their strength to the hinds by thrashing their antlers against the tree stems. Low vegetation is eaten, and woodland edges or overgrown hedges often have a distinctive browse line about two metres above the ground, marking the limits of the deer's reach.

When they pass through hedge-banks along the lanes, there are 'up and overs'. The deer use the same routes repeatedly and the hooves of such a heavy animal cut deeply into the soil. They turn these crossing points to mud in winter, spilling stones onto the lane below and pushing their way through what was once a secure, stockproof barrier. The local farmers resort to shoving wooden palettes into the gaps or even tying short sections of electric-fence wire across the holes. The wire is no obstacle to the deer but cattle know from experience what it looks (and feels) like and, unlike deer, they don't have the dexterity to leap over. They also lack the common sense to work out that there is no battery nearby. It seems to work well enough.

The Red Deer is the one wild animal that makes trails useful for humans and I often follow one when trying to pick out a route across unfamiliar terrain. They avoid the boggiest ground, push narrow gaps through dense bushes, and converge on the weak points in hedges and fence lines; there is no point in jumping a fence if a fallen branch has flattened it a little further ahead. The deer conserve their energy and I'm happy to follow suit.

Frequent muddy wallows are another regular feature of woodland where Red Deer are common. I retain an unfulfilled ambition to see a deer actually using one, and I guess this must happen mostly after dark when they feel more secure. But the results are all too obvious.

Deer leave their long hairs on all three strands of a typical barbed-wire fence. This is because, if they are under no pressure, they will casually step through between the wires when passing from one side to the other. If they are in more of a hurry they will leap over the top, usually with nonchalant ease, although occasionally they come unstuck. Not far from our house I once found a buck Roe Deer hanging dead from the top of a stock fence between two fields. It had tried to jump over but must have clipped the top, and two wires close together had ensnared its hind leg, holding it in a vice-like grip. It was there for months, gradually decaying to skin and bone, protected from all but the most determined scavengers by its precarious position.

One mammal, above all others, is known for the signs it leaves. It is not one I've ever thought to look out for in mid-Devon, but that all changed a few months ago. Early one morning, I was approaching an isolated pond in a remote spot on a private estate. I'd been here a few times before but today it looked different somehow. I couldn't put my finger on it but perhaps it was a little more open than before, with fewer trees and bushes. The landowner must have cleared some vegetation to make the pond more accessible, I decided. I walked closer and all became clear. The landowner had indeed made some changes, but rather than felling the trees himself he had brought in something to do it for him.

What was once a fringe of birches and willows was now a ruin of criss-crossed, horizontal trunks. The largest trees, up to a foot or more in diameter, were still works in progress, but sufficient inroads had been made to suggest they too would succumb in the end. White flakes of wood littered the ground and I picked one up instinctively – evidence for any non-believers when I came to tell the story later. On the far side of the pond, where it once drained into a small stream, sticks and mud had been piled up at least two metres high, raising the level of the water. Having got over my surprise I sat quietly against one of the few surviving trees and waited. Sure enough, after a few minutes, a low shape appeared at the surface. It swam from one side of the pond to the other, before slipping quietly under the water as it neared the dam.

I'd seen my first ever Beaver in the wild in Britain, but I came away with mixed feelings about the experience. Hopefully, as this animal returns to our countryside after its long absence, it will regain a sense of 'wildness' that was somehow missing today. I couldn't quite get past the knowledge that the animals present here had been installed (almost certainly illegally) by humans, and had been bred or imported specially for the purpose. These Beavers carried the taint of captivity and the fact that decisions were made *for* them rather than *by* them. Time will be needed before they become as wild as the Red Deer, Foxes and Badgers with which they now share the landscape.

Birds are usually easier to watch than mammals but the signs they leave behind are still invaluable. I've seen Goshawks close to the house many times, as we are lucky enough to have a nest site in the adjacent wood. I've watched them hunt and occasionally seen them attempt to catch something. But I've yet to see them make a kill and were it not for the remains they leave behind, I'd have no idea what they eat. An autumn visit to the nest, after the young have fledged and moved away, is especially instructive. Bones and feathers litter the ground below, showing that Tawny Owl, Jay, Woodpigeon, Pheasant, Grey Squirrel and Rabbit have all been on the menu.

Owls go one better. They leave a near complete record of everything they eat. Prey is usually swallowed whole, digested and then the hard parts along with the fur and feathers are coughed up in a pellet. I regularly walk by an old cobb-walled farm, long since abandoned and now under siege from brambles. This open-fronted building often has pellets and moulted feathers lying on the dusty floor below. I occasionally collect a few pellets and wash out the skulls and bones to see what the owls have been eating. I was about to do just that one day and was looking down at the floor when a grey cylinder suddenly landed right in front of me and settled in the dust. As I looked up, a Barn Owl, now just a little lighter, raised its wings, and then lifted from the ancient wooden rafters and headed off into the daylight.

Raptor pellets are a handy, non-invasive way of surveying small mammals that are otherwise difficult to detect. As expected, our local Barn Owls eat mainly Field Voles, but I've also found the skulls of Common Shrew, Bank Vole, Wood Mouse and young Brown Rat. In Ireland, a mammal previously unknown to these islands was recently discovered from remains found in a Barn Owl pellet.* The Greater White-toothed Shrew turned out to be quite common locally but until that point it had gone unnoticed by humans, if not by the local birds of prey.

We humans, of course, leave far more traces of our presence than any other animal. A feature of even the more remote woods in this area is the old dumps along the edges, some of them miles from the nearest building. Before the days of organised refuse collections, each local farm would have had a place where rubbish was disposed of. Carting it to the edge of the nearest wood and slinging it over the fence at least kept it out of sight. These dumps are now overgrown with vegetation and much has been swallowed by the soil. But a little poking around offers a glimpse into the past: I've found rusty buckets, tin baths, coal

---

* Tosh, D. G. *et al.* (2008) First record of Greater White-toothed Shrew *Crocidura russula* in Ireland. *Mammal Review* 38: 321–26.

scuttles, cast-iron kettles, a decaying Rover 10 sports tourer from before the war, and wonderful, old metal milk churns from a time before lorries with huge tanks made them redundant. I sometimes manage to retrieve a glass bottle or two and have built up a little collection of old ink pots, milk bottles, Marmite jars, and the distinctive blue glass bottles once used for poisons.

My best bottle find to date was a complete surprise. I was walking the dog along the lane near home and there it was, lying out in the open at the base of the hedge: a green glass codd bottle, complete with the marble that once helped seal in the drink. It must be at least a century old and yet it looked as if it had been tossed from a passing car that morning. These bottles carried a deposit and would be returned to the shop to be reused. Presumably it had been left in the hedge by mistake, perhaps by a farm worker; maybe it was forgotten as he moved along the bank, methodically cutting and laying the woody stems. It would no doubt have quickly been covered by leaves, new growth and then soil. Erosion had now revealed it once again, and out it rolled, down the bank and onto the verge. I picked it up and wiped away a little dirt: 'B H BREARLEY' of 'SOUTH MOLTON'; and he was still not going to get his bottle back.

Trying to read signs in the landscape is a reminder of the natural and anthropogenic processes operating all around us, on vastly different timescales: hedges planted centuries ago and maintained over generations; deer that have, down the years, managed to breach them as they move from place to place, following their routes and routines; a fresh fall of earth and stones from the hedge bank where the deer passed through just last night – and perhaps dislodged the bottle of a hedge-layer, long dead. It has become popular to seek time in nature in the mindful present; to appreciate birds singing, the rustle of leaves underfoot and the breeze stirring among the branches. But the context of history is always informative, whether that is over the last few hours, years, decades or centuries.

FELLOW-TRAVELLERS

People often build strong bonds with well-loved and familiar places. The word 'place' itself helps to suggest why this is, as explained by artist Alan Gussow:

> The catalyst that converts any physical location – any environment if you will – into a place, is the process of experiencing deeply. A place is a piece of a whole environment that has been claimed by feelings.[*]

In his book *Irreplaceable*, Julian Hoffman expands on this, pointing out that 'places which are held dear instil feelings of joy, calm, peace, rejuvenation, security and belonging'. He goes on to highlight studies based on MRI brain scans showing that 'significant places spark greater emotional resonance in people than personally valued objects, a particularly surprising find in a largely material culture'.[†]

---

[*] Gussow, A. (1997) *A Sense of Place: The Artist and the American Land*. Island Press, Washington.
[†] Hoffman, J. (2019) *Irreplaceable: The Fight to Save our Wild Places*. Penguin Books, London.

Perhaps because I've moved around the country a lot, I've found it difficult to forge meaningful, lasting connections with place. Instead, it's my bonds with individual species that run deepest and have stood the test of time. A plant or animal that is common and widespread in the landscape can follow you around on your travels, even as your favourite places are left far behind. I understand what Gussow and Hoffman are getting at, but I want to replace 'physical location', 'environment' and 'place' in their quotes with references to species, animals and plants.

As an ornithologist, most of my 'special' species are birds. I've written elsewhere about the Wren.* It's my favourite fellow-traveller, a bird that is capable of soothing a troubled soul almost anywhere in Britain. This species is familiar from our gardens, parks and urban areas, but it will also appear if you venture into dense woodland, cross open expanses of moorland, climb our highest mountains or find your way to our remotest island outposts. Wherever there are trees, or bushes, or rocks, in summer or in winter, the humble Wren will be there, scratching out an existence. And, in summer at least, its explosive song means that you are unlikely to miss it, despite its small size and unobtrusive behaviour. It wouldn't be ethical, but if you are carrying out bird surveys almost anywhere in Britain this is a species you could add to your recording sheet before you begin to walk your transect.

For Stephen Rutt, with his love of seabirds, it's the Fulmar that offers familiarity and connection as he travels around Britain's coast and islands:

---

* See Carter, I. (2021) *Human, Nature*, pp. 44–48.

Birds are bridges. I found Fulmars everywhere on my journey, ghosting along shorelines in effortless flight. They make me feel at home, regardless of how distant the ground under my feet is.*

If I were told I could never again visit the local common, or any of my other favourite wildlife sites, I'd come to terms with the news pretty quickly. But if I were not allowed to see another Wren, or Rook, or House Sparrow – or, come to think of it, another Fulmar. Well… that would be tough to take.

A few plants also make it onto my 'specials' list, and I can travel further back through time with one of them than with any bird. This plant needs a certain amount of light to do well, so it favours open habitats, but it can make do in woodland provided the canopy is not too dense. Where it thrives, it changes the character of the land. On open ground it may be so dominant that it's often considered as a habitat in its own right, one that is not welcomed by everyone; there is reedbed, grassland, heathland – and then there is Bracken.

In autumn the bright green fronds fade to yellow and then brown, as the head-high stems begin to fold and crumple. Different individual plants change at different rates, providing an ever-shifting mix of colours and textures. In woodland, Bracken seems to reflect the changing colour of the trees high overhead. And as autumn proceeds, the two come together as the tree leaves fall.

* Rutt, S. (2019) *The Seafarers: A Journey Among Birds*. Elliot and Thompson, London.

The dense foliage takes a while to die back, but by midwinter the plants lie limp and broken on the ground. The process of decay takes hold and the fern loses its grip on the land for the coldest months of the year. Then, in early spring, delicate grey-green, 'fiddlehead' shoots begin to push up through the leaf-litter as the cycle begins once more.

Bracken has some practical uses as well as being aesthetically pleasing. It doesn't like getting its feet wet, so if you feel the same way it's a good plant to look out for. On open expanses of moor and rough grassland it maps the driest patches of land. By scanning ahead and seeking out the patches of Bracken, you can avoid the most treacherous, waterlogged places.

It was once highly valued as an easily gathered, soft and absorbent bedding for livestock, and it was also employed in thatch for livestock shelters. Local people had the legal right to harvest Bracken from common land, and that no doubt helped to keep it in check. This is a plant that connects us with our history and the way we once worked with, rather than against, wild places. Today it is still occasionally put to good use by being cut and made into potting compost or even 'brackette' logs for the fire.

Bracken helps connect me to my own history. Whenever I see an expanse of it growing in woodland I'm drawn back to early childhood and the hours I once spent playing within its forest of fronds. There was a lightly wooded hillside within a few minutes of home. Every spring, a jungle of foliage would rise up, transforming the slope into an irresistible outdoor playground. By flattening the plants in a small square of land, our 'gang' could create an instant hiding place, screened from the adult world (and imaginary rival gangs) by lush, tall greenery. We'd make many of these hideouts across the slope, connecting them via narrow pathways beneath a roof of arching leaves – our own secret network. The ferns could even be fashioned into weapons to defend our hideouts. By stripping the side branches and leaving just a short sprig of leaves at the top, the stiff stems made serviceable spears, held true by the tuft of leaves, like the feathers on an arrow. Do kids still do this sort of thing I wonder?

Bracken is not everybody's cup of tea of course. It can be invasive and it sometimes spreads inexorably across habitats that we value highly, shading out the plants beneath. It produces toxins that inhibit the growth of other species, and it can make livestock sick if they resort to eating it. In some countries the young shoots are still eaten by people, though this too comes with a serious health warning as they contain known carcinogens. A search online will soon reveal outpourings of hatred against Bracken, and contractors lining up with offers to eradicate it. Some will even take to the skies to spray herbicide in order to rid the land of this plant.

There is another plant capable of covering large areas of ground, mostly within woodland. It shares Bracken's ability to dominate at the expense of other species, and it too contains toxins that deter attack from insects and other herbivores. All parts of the plant are poisonous and dogs are at risk if they inadvertently ingest the bulbs when digging in the soil. Unlike Bracken it has no practical uses, though a handful brought indoors will certainly brighten up a room. What sets it apart from Bracken, and assures it of a place in our affections, are its flowers; a plant that creates a vibrant haze of blue in the spring is universally welcomed, and so we turn a blind eye to its ability to outcompete other plants.

When our family moved south from Cheshire to Oxfordshire in the early 1980s, the woods adjoining the garden had a carpet of Bluebells. In late winter, the leaves would begin, once again, to push up through the leaf-litter, spearing through decaying leaves, lifting them clear of the ground. The muted brown of the woodland floor was slowly erased, becoming green and then, gloriously, blue. My mum would keep a watchful eye on the unfolding scene on her daily dog walk. Any plant threatening to grow up and spoil the monoculture was shown no mercy. Nothing was allowed to detract from 'the blue buzzed-haze and the wafts of intoxicant perfume' that so enraptured Gerard Manley Hopkins.

Britain and Ireland apparently have more Bluebells than the rest of the world combined. It has been suggested that the absence of the Wild Boar, hunted to extinction here long ago, may have helped it to establish the unbroken carpets of plants that we have come, so much, to love. Boar rootle into the earth with their snouts when foraging. When they were common this would have damaged and dislodged Bluebell bulbs, as well as providing fresh earth where other plants could become established. If Wild Boar continue to recolonise, having escaped from commercial farms, the spectacle of massed ranks of Bluebells may be diminished in future, replaced by a more diverse (and arguably more natural) assemblage of plants on the woodland floor.

On our local common here in Devon there are small patches where Bracken and Bluebells come together in the spring, showing that, just occasionally, harmony is possible. The Bracken forms a miniature forest of fronds, shading the ground and stifling competition from the otherwise dominant grasses. Here, plants more typical of woodland and hedgerow can find space. There are Bluebells, as well as Lesser Celandine, Red Campion, stitchwort and violets growing beneath the protective canopy – vibrant splashes of blue, yellow, red, white and pink, offering a welcome contrast to the pale straw of dead grasses across the rest of the moor. When the sun comes out, delicate Small Pearl-bordered Fritillary butterflies appear, adding bright orange to the palette as they bask on the Bracken fronds or seek out the leaves of violets on which to lay their eggs.

Our dog sometimes disappears inside dense Bracken beds, weaving between the wiry stems, exploring a hidden world. Occasionally, while I wait, I'll lie back on the ground, hemmed in by the soft green foliage. And I'll dream of that distant hillside, and the ghosts of its long-forgotten gang of small boys, defending their territory with Bracken-stem spears.

WILD BROWSING

An interest in wild food was instilled within me in early childhood. Then, there were regular family outings to search the woods for hazelnuts and sweet chestnuts, or to walk the lanes filling old ice-cream tubs with blackberries. Nuts and berries were there in abundance and we were taught that it would be wasteful to ignore them. Gathering food became a traditional autumn activity, though with reminders that lasted well into winter: deep scratches on the arms from the bramble thorns, and blackberries and ice cream for pudding.

My cooking skills are sorely lacking, so – with a few exceptions – I tend to browse and graze in the field rather than bring food back to the kitchen. I admire people who return home with armfuls of natural produce and busy themselves turning it into meals, preserves and drinks. But, despite the lessons from childhood, that's not really my thing. I do, though, enjoy knowing what can be gleaned on a local walk and I'm constantly picking things to snack on. I don't have many walks, even in midwinter, when at least one plant isn't sampled, more through habit than hunger. Sometimes I'll fill a pocket with nuts or berries that can be taken home to be eaten over the following few days. Less often, I'll gather something that has to be cooked but only if it conforms to my slothful (but sacrosanct) 'ten-minute rule'. These foods need some basic preparation back at home before they can be eaten but this is straightforward and can be done within the time allowed. Not many things make the cut.

The benefits of eating wild plants extend to far more than the food itself. For me, it's more about the connection this brings with the local landscape. There is something remarkably life affirming about the act of picking and eating things that you have tracked down and identified for yourself. This presumably stems from the hunter-gatherer instinct that is there, somewhere, in all of us. For obvious reasons it's an extremely powerful trait, though it can take some re-finding in our frenetically busy and detached world. It leads some people to shoot hand-reared gamebirds from the sky, but it can be used more constructively too.

There is, of course, a connection when watching (rather than eating) wildlife but it doesn't run nearly so deep. When you have foraging on your mind you become more intensely aware of subtle seasonal changes as different species rise in prominence and then fade from the scene for another year. A good autumn for Chanterelle fungi is more memorable to me than, say, a good autumn for Red Admirals because it is reinforced through the processes of searching, harvesting and consuming. This is hands-on and it engages more of the senses – all of them in fact, with smell being important to identify certain plants and fungi. It also pulls me back to the same places year after year, hoping for more of the same. And it helps me to appreciate year to year variations, and to ponder the reasons behind them.

There are other benefits that are simply not available by any other means – at any price. Much as people who grow their own vegetables struggle with the taste of shop-bought produce, the same is true with wild food. Try replicating the taste of Parasol mushrooms, gathered in their prime from a local grassland and on the plate within the hour. Or how about fresh hazelnuts pulled down by hand from the yellowing autumn foliage. A trip to the supermarket won't help. You can't buy the Parasols and whilst you might find the nuts, they'll be a domesticated version and will have been lying around in a dusty warehouse, or on the shelves, for who knows how many weeks.

Questions are sometimes raised about the impacts of harvesting on wildlife and on the enjoyment of other people. While this hardly applies to a little harmless browsing, it's worth pausing to consider. There is an awful lot of untapped wild food out there and a great deal more use could be made of it before there is any serious threat of depletion. Nevertheless, a little common sense is useful. Clearing a field full of spectacular, plate-sized Parasols, and thus depriving others of the opportunity to see them, is not really on. But taking one home for tea feels perfectly reasonable. Stripping a small patch of brambles or Hazel trees of every last fruit or nut is questionable. Taking a few from a long hedgerow so that no-one would even know you'd visited is surely not a problem.

Removing food from the countryside can clearly have impacts on wildlife – some of them negative. After all, it is sustenance for other creatures too. The litmus test for foraging is not whether there are no impacts, but whether the impacts are lower than the alternatives. These vary hugely, but I'd be confident that locally sourced wild food comes out on the right side of the equation 99 per cent of the time when compared with the closest super-market equivalent. Anything gathered close to home or collected opportunistically when out and about doing other things has a food mileage of zero. In eating it, you are reducing consumption of shop-bought food with levels of sustainability ranging from tolerable to ludicrous.

As with anything, the actions of any one individual have only a tiny impact on the way the world works. But they do make a difference, and if you can persuade a few others to join you, that helps all the more. I'm reminded of something George Monbiot wrote about the benefits of trying to act positively rather than giving up in despair (in respect of climate change, but the same applies here). Why should individuals even bother trying to minimise their impacts when global behaviour patterns mean we will inevitably lose much of what we hold dear? Well, if all we can do is help to 'draw out the losses over as long a period as possible, in order to allow our children and grandchildren to experience something of the wonder and delight in the natural world ... is that not a worthy aim, even if there were no other?'* Wild food can help with that, in a tiny, but nevertheless worthwhile, way.

Before taking the plunge it's important to keep in mind that, contrary to the many advertising slogans, 'natural' does not always equate to 'beneficial'. Plants have been defending themselves against herbivores for generations and have come up with an impressive armoury of chemicals for protection. Ironically, some of these deterrents are what gives a plant its appealing taste (see Wild Garlic below); they can be effective against many animals, while having no adverse effects on humans. Equally, there are

---

* Monbiot, G. (2016) *How Did We Get Into this Mess: Politics, Equality, Nature.* Verso, London.

plants and fungi that are much nibbled by wild animals –
something that was once taken as a sign they were good to eat
– but are lethally toxic to humans. For us they may be edible,
but only once, as the old saying goes.

Some poisonous plants will kill you quickly, others result in
protracted period of indescribably gruesome symptoms before
the welcome release of death. There are fungi that are fine to eat
unless consumed at the same time as alcohol. Others are poisonous
when raw but good to eat after cooking. And a few seem fine
when eaten the first few times but result in a gradual build-up
of toxins which take effect only after an invisible and unknowable
threshold has been reached. Then there are the species that were
once considered edible but for which recent research has called
that into question. Comfrey was a plant much used in herbal
remedies and is still listed as edible in some books; however, it
is now thought that it can result in serious liver damage.

Even useful plants must be treated with respect. Foxgloves
contain the chemical digitalis, which in a carefully measured dose
is used to regulate heart function. But eat a few leaves and it
will stop, rather than slow, your heart. Deadly Nightshade is
another lethally poisonous plant and has attractive, shiny black
berries that could easily tempt the unwary. The toxin, atropine,
causes the heart rate to increase. Overdose on digitalis from
Foxgloves and atropine from Deadly Nightshade might just save
you, but get the balance slightly wrong and they will be the last
things you eat. A few plants are so toxic that even skin contact
can be a problem. Children have been poisoned by appropriating
the stems of the toxic Hemlock for use as pea-shooters. And
certain fungi are so poisonous that careless handling can cause

illness, or worse, if other foods are then consumed before hand-washing.

Such a wide range of different effects may seem surprising, until you consider the evolutionary history. Plants and fungi have lived alongside animals, including humans, for millions of years, over which time a complex web of interactions and effects has developed. Plants sometimes make use of animals to help disperse their seeds. They offer us a tasty edible coating in the hope that we will consume the berry and deposit the seed elsewhere with a handy dollop of fertiliser. But they also defend themselves when necessary, by physical means such as hard shells, spines and prickly leaves, or through chemical warfare.

If you think you might like to dabble in wild foods, the plants and fungi mentioned below are perfect species to start with. They are all common and widespread, not too difficult to find or identify, and taken together provide something to target all year-round. It's worth stressing that you don't need to be an expert. If you can learn just a handful of species to start off, your walks will begin to provide added interest, and a little healthy food to go with the exercise. If you're unfamiliar with the plants below, then a decent book (or website) will be needed to get started but each one can be learnt in just a few minutes. Most of these species can be eaten raw when out and about, but the final few sneak in through the (non-negotiable) ten-minute rule.

Hairy Bitter-cress

This low-growing and unassuming plant has quite a bit going for it and is well worth the effort to learn. It has the delightful habit of bringing wild food to your back door as it often grows as a garden weed, springing up in flowerpots, the gaps between patio paving slabs or around the edges of flowerbeds. It's often available year-round, emerging in early spring and seeding itself right through the winter if conditions remain mild.

It doesn't entirely live up to its name in that it's not especially hairy and it doesn't taste bitter, though the 'cress' part, at least, is spot on. It can be used in salads or in sandwiches and I find it a great fall-back for days when I haven't been able to get out into the countryside. I can wander into the garden at lunchtime and brighten up a cheese sandwich with a sprinkling of leaves. The elongated seed pods are also edible, though the tiny seeds are eaten by small finches and other species, so leave some in place if you want to attract birds to your garden. There are a few similar but less common bitter-cresses and the well-known pink-bloomed Cuckooflower (or Lady's Smock) is also part of the same group. All are edible, with varying degrees of spiciness, so a bit of experimentation is worthwhile.

Wood-sorrel

This small, delicate and distinctive plant is easy to overlook with its diminutive stature and uniform pale-green colour, but once you start looking, you'll begin to notice it regularly. The heart-shaped leaves can be found throughout the year in a wide range of habitats, though it is less common, and the leaves drier and tougher, during the winter months. Occasionally it carpets small areas of ancient woodland and when the delicately pink-lined, white flowers emerge, often around Easter, they make an attractive display.

Closely related plants in North America are known as 'sour grass' and that gives a clue to the taste. The small leaves have a surprisingly strong, sharp tang to them, not unlike lemons though not so overpowering. I've never been more adventurous than to graze on the leaves during a walk but you could use them in salads to liven them up a bit, or even try adding them to more savoury dishes to enhance the flavour. The leaves are high in vitamin C.

Common Sorrel

Many common garden 'weeds' are technically edible but hard to get excited about. The Dandelion is perhaps the most abundant and is no doubt very good for you but the leaves are undeniably bland. Common Sorrel, another widespread grassland plant prone to appearing on unkempt lawns, at least has a bit of bite to it. The taste of the fresh leaves is often likened to apple peel – pleasant enough, if rather chewy and with a slightly acidic kick.

This plant is in the Dock family and unrelated to Wood-sorrel, despite the fact that the species share an acidic taste: they both contain oxalic acid, presumably as a defence against insect pests and grazing animals. It can also be toxic for humans but only in quantities sufficiently large that the casual forager need have no concerns.

The leaves of Common Sorrel are distinctive once you get your eye in, being arrow-shaped with obvious pointed lobes at the base. The closely related Sheep's Sorrel looks similar, is also edible and tastes much the same. The leaves are mostly green, but a few become tinged with red, as if anticipating the autumn.

They are found throughout the year, providing something to chew on even in midwinter when not much else is available.

Wild Garlic

Wild Garlic, or Ramsons as it's sometimes called, is one of the most eagerly awaited plants of the spring for its aesthetic appeal as well as its flavour. It has become very trendy in restaurants in recent years as more and more chefs tap into the popularity of wild food. By late April it carpets the floor of ancient woodland where conditions are right, a haze of white flowers floating above the longer-established green leaves. It's often found in the same place as Bluebells, and the flowers usually peak at about the same time, producing a dazzling display.

All parts of the plant are edible, though it's usually the leaves that are harvested. They are at their best in the early spring when newly emerged and tender. The strong garlic smell is most apparent when the leaves are crushed but you sometimes catch a hint of it even before you've entered the wood. The scent is handy for confirming the identification, as some superficially similar spring plants contain unpleasant toxins for self-defence; they are emerging at a time of year when any fresh growth is highly appealing to herbivores worn down by the rigours of winter.

The way the scent of garlic is released on crushing suggests that this too is a defence mechanism, deployed to its fullest extent when the plant is under attack. It seems to be very successful, judging by the dominance of the plant in favoured locations. It works well in deterring some humans too – though for those who do enjoy eating it, it is beneficial rather than harmful, acting as an antioxidant and apparently helping to reduce cholesterol levels. It is also reputed to lower blood pressure, as does the stroll through the woods to find it.

The taste is less overpowering than garlic from the supermarket and goes especially well with tomato and cheese. Try a few leaves in a sandwich and you might find yourself adopting a new annual ritual in early March, scouring your local woods for the first fresh leaves of the year.

Mint

The smell of mint induces a feeling of nostalgia that no other plant can match. One of the few jobs I was trusted not to mess up as a small child was to go out into the back garden to gather a few mint leaves for the Sunday roast. It must have been the first plant I learnt to recognise and put a name to; fifty years on the scent still takes me back to those hazy, faraway days.

There are a number of different wild mint species that all look rather similar, especially before they begin to flower. They also hybridise readily which makes things even more complicated. As a non-botanist I'm afraid I tend to lump them all together. Thankfully, so long as your plant looks and, equally important, smells like mint then it is safe to use.

As well as its traditional use to bring out the flavour in roast lamb, the leaves make a refreshing drink. It's a nice way to end a walk if you can locate a handy patch of plants as you near home. Just nip off the uppermost whorls of leaves from two or three plants and add recently boiled water. The flavour intensifies as the leaves continue to stew, so remove them once you have a drink that suits.

Wild Strawberry

'Doubtless God could have made a better berry, but doubtless God never did.' So said a Dr William Butler in the seventeenth century and, some 400 years later, it's hard to argue with him.*
This is a delightful plant, with delicate white flowers and, if your luck is in, irresistible red berries. The plant is a diminutive version of the familiar cultivated strawberry and so identification poses few problems. It tends to grow in small clumps and favours poor soils where it is not swamped by more vigorous competitors. In much of our nutrient-soaked countryside it risks drowning in a sea of tall grasses and Cow Parsley, and the berries can be hidden from view even if the plants cling to survival.

Wild Strawberry fruits are often available for just a few weeks each year in any one place (which adds to their appeal), though a longer season is possible if you can find them growing in different situations. Much like Bluebells and Primroses, plants growing within the shade of woodland can be well behind those in a more open situation.

The taste is just what you'd expect from a strawberry and more than a match for the cultivated equivalent. If it has a problem it's the tiny size of the fruits. Perhaps 10 or 12 would be needed to match the volume of just one typically sized supermarket strawberry. This makes it difficult to gather them in meaningful amounts, but they are perfect for snacking on.

---

* This quote is taken from one of John Wright's indispensible books on wild food: Wright, J. (2010) *The River Cottage Hedgerow Handbook*. Bloomsbury, London.

Blackberry

There can't be many people who haven't picked and eaten this fruit at one time or another. After all, we have been eating them for a long time; the seeds have been found in human remains unearthed from the Bronze Age, over 3,000 years ago. Modern parents who are wary (or unaware) of almost all other forms of wild food will happily send their kids out blackberrying. The bushes have a knack for brightening up places that are otherwise dull and lacking in alternative wild foods. Even in urban areas and the most intensively managed farmland, an exploratory walk is likely to turn up a bush or two.

The berries have a long season. The pioneers ripen as early as June in some years and can then be found well into the early winter in mild conditions, though the taste tends to deteriorate late in the season. Some blame the Devil for spitting on them on Michaelmas day (29 September) but flies and autumn moulds are the more likely explanation. It's not just humans that relish blackberries. Insects, birds and small mammals all take advantage. I once watched a Roe Deer working along a hedgerow, pausing often to delicately select and remove the sweetest, ripest berry from the end of each shoot. Our Cocker Spaniel has learnt the same trick. Now, when I stop to pick berries, she breaks from her walk too, hoping for some low-hanging fruit.

Rather like exotically coloured but commonplace garden birds such as the Blue Tit and Great Tit, you suspect our appreciation for blackberries has been dulled by their ubiquity. The human brain relishes a challenge and something that is ridiculously easy to find becomes less appreciated, however good it looks or tastes.

Wild Raspberry

Although not so common or noticeable as the blackberry, this plant can be found widely across the country in sunny woodland clearings and along tangled hedgerows. The plants produce fruits that are similar to the cultivated varieties, though they are usually smaller. The similarity leads people to believe they are escapes from cultivation, even when found well away from civilisation. On the contrary, this is a genuinely wild, native plant, with a long history, and is all the more enjoyable for that.

The plants are not defended as heavily as brambles and the small thorns are less likely than their thuggish relative to shred your skin, or even your clothes, during the gathering process. Another advantage is their early season. The fruits often ripen ahead of the blackberry. Where the two plants grow together, ripe raspberries can hide in plain sight, masquerading as unripe red blackberries.

Hazelnut

This is one of my favourite wild foods. Between early August and October (in a good year) I don't go for many local walks without risking my teeth and cracking open at least one or two. A good test as to whether the nuts are ripe enough to be worth collecting is to try to squeeze them out from their holders. If they slip out into your hand then they are ready. My dad tells me that kids in his day referred to them as 'slippers' for this reason; a quick online search for this term found nothing but footwear, so I presume it was local Gloucestershire slang rather than in wider use. The nuts keep well, easily lasting until Christmas and beyond, and the taste changes subtly as they age – they lose some of their crunchiness as they dry out, and become slightly sweeter.

The Hazel would have been one of the first trees to recolonise Britain following the last ice age and it's easy to feel something of a connection with ancient landscapes when eating the nuts: animals (including people) have been doing the same thing, in much the same places, for thousands of years.

In modern Britain too, you will likely face some stiff competition – so much so that it's a rare treat to find a fully ripe, deep-brown coloured nut in October. Usually, you must gather them earlier in the season when the shells still have some green in them, though they taste delicious nonetheless. It's not fellow humans that are pinching them these days. Rather, it's the introduced Grey Squirrel that does the damage. If you are too late reaching the trees, they will be bare, the nuts transformed into a dispiriting clutter of split shells on the ground below.

Grey Squirrels are so effective at stripping Hazels that this surely has impacts on native species that also enjoy these nuts – the declining Common Dormouse for example. It also makes me wonder whether our native Red Squirrels were just as efficient at nut harvesting before they were pushed out by the Greys?

Sweet Chestnut

This is not a native tree but it has been established in Britain for around 2,000 years and the nuts have long been exploited by humans. They only ripen well in certain years and, even then, only on a subset of the mature trees – so if the first tree is unproductive don't give up. Climate change may help in future, as the tree's native range includes southern Europe and North Africa.

The nuts tend to ripen and fall from the trees in late autumn and can be found well into November, when most other fruits and nuts are over. I can't resist eating them raw, though they have a slightly dry and bitter taste. It's best to scrape away the fibrous coating after removing the glossy-brown shell or it can be like trying to chew through a mouthful of fluff. If they are still in their green outer cases then gloves (or a stout boot) will be needed to release them; the prickles have been superbly well honed by evolution, making them almost impossible to handle.

Traditionally, of course, chestnuts are roasted over a fire, with holes pricked into the shell to help the heating process and release the hot gas that otherwise builds up inside. A neat trick to help gauge when they are ready is to leave one or two with un-pricked shells. When these explode, the rest are ready to eat. This rarely works perfectly but is a great way to keep a room full of drowsy Christmas visitors on their toes.

Sloes

I do admire people who produce their own wine from flowers, fruits or leaves gleaned from the countryside. It seems to require lots of faffing about with all sorts of different ingredients, and endless decanting of fluids from one vessel to another – followed by a long, nerve-wracking wait to see if it has worked. I'm sure, once you get the hang of things, it's easier than it appears. But in case you never do, I'd recommend sloe gin (or even sloe vodka) as an altogether simpler alternative.

Making sloe gin really is as easy as picking the sloes in the autumn, adding them to a jar or bottle and tipping some gin on top. Unlike in wine-making, there is very little that can go wrong. If the sloes are still hard when picked then it's worth pricking them to help allow the flavour to seep out. Some people spike them with one of the defensive thorns, handily provided by the Blackthorn bushes, as they are picked. Alternatively, you can wait until after the first significant frost has done the work for you by softening the fruits, though these days it may come too late, when the berries have already shrivelled and become unusable. If you add sugar and perhaps a drop of almond essence to the mix when you start, it will sweeten the end product.

Ideally, sloe gin needs to be left for a few months at least and the longer you resist temptation, the more the flavour and the rich purple colour intensifies. Making it in October for Christmas is fine if the holiday spirit means you can wait no longer. But try leaving at least one bottle for a full six months, or even until the following Christmas, just to experience the difference. If you've ever tasted the sour fruits straight from the tree, you'll be amazed that such a rich and pleasant flavour could possibly be lurking within them.

Parasol mushroom

Picking mushrooms, or fungi, is not dissimilar to foraging for apples or blackberries in that you are removing a few of the reproductive structures but leaving the main body of the organism safely intact. Parasols make for an impressive sight when they grow in numbers. At first, they look like chicken drumsticks but gradually the cap develops and flattens out, sometimes approaching a small dinner-plate in size, the tall stems making them visible from a distance. Once the caps have expanded to their full size it's hard to confuse them with any other species.

You can eat the caps raw but cooking is the best option. My culinary skills don't extend much beyond 'putting things on toast', so these are perfect. They don't even need to be cut up if you can find a nice slice-of-bread sized specimen, and they have a strong, nutty flavour. Preparation involves nothing more than wiping them clean, discarding the tough stem, and adding to a frying pan with a knob of butter and perhaps a garlic clove or two.

Puffballs

There are a few different species of puffball, ranging in size from the small, spiny, Common Puffball and its close relatives, to the altogether more impressive, football-sized Giant Puffball. The stalks are often hidden underground, leaving just the rotund fruiting body visible from above. The good news is that all the similar-looking species are edible, so the subtle differences between them aren't worth worrying about – unless you enjoy worrying about such things. Do, though, watch out for the superficially similar earth-balls which have tougher, thicker, scaly skins and an off-white (rather than pure white) inner flesh, even when young.

The smaller puffballs are very common and while they may not be the tastiest of wild fungi they are still preferable to most shop-bought varieties. They are only good to eat when young, when the flesh inside is still white. As they mature and the spores ripen, the flesh dries out and starts to yellow, eventually reaching the final 'puffing' phase which gives them their name. These are the familiar brown papery structures that children (and adults) can't resist stamping on to send a dark puff of spores shooting into the air. This might seem a bit mindless, but it's helping to secure the future of the species so don't feel bad about it. If an accommodating human doesn't find them, passing animals or even drops of rain will hopefully do the same job.

If you find a promising group of puffballs it's worth cutting one open in the field just to check that it's still young enough to eat. That avoids the risk of harvesting a batch only to find, once you get home, that they are all past their best. If you have the patience, you can peel off the outer skins before cooking as they are much tougher than the flesh inside and a little too chewy for the more discerning palate.

Chanterelle

I've left this one until last because it's a little more challenging to find and identify. The effort, though, is well worthwhile. This is perhaps the finest of all our wild fungi. On the continent, people have been known to come to blows over a profitable patch of Chanterelles, though in my local Devon countryside I've yet to encounter anyone else with the slightest interest in them – which is fine with me.

When it comes to finding them, the fact that they are bright yellow-orange is helpful. On a gloomy day in woodland they seem to glow up from the leaf-litter and can be spotted from a distance. Sometimes I pick up their soft scent of apricots before I've seen them, and this is a useful test to make sure of the identification. Try searching in woods with oak, beech or pine trees between August and October, and look along ditches or hedge-banks rather than wandering into the middle of a large expanse of forest.

These mushrooms take just a few minutes to turn into lunch: cooking them is as simple as adding butter and garlic to a frying pan, cleaning away any obvious dirt and lobbing them in – small ones whole, larger ones cut into pieces. Then just put them on toast. If you don't like the result then you will have found out something useful: foraging for wild fungi of any kind is probably not for you.

WAYS OF SEEING

REMINDERS OF WILDERNESS

I find that the wilder a place feels, the more relaxing the time spent there. A few minutes in an urban green space is one thing – and should not be undervalued – but a walk in a location where few reminders of humanity are apparent and natural processes dominate is an altogether more rewarding experience. Throughout my life I've kept this firmly in mind whenever I visit a new area. Seeking out the wildest corners that a landscape can offer has become a minor obsession – an ongoing quest to find places where signs of human influence fall away, leaving a natural (or apparently natural) setting.

In other parts of the world I've had the pleasure of experiencing true wilderness, or as close as it's possible to get to it these days. Some of the national parks in the USA and Canada protect vast areas of mountain and forest that are close to their natural state. It is possible to walk deep into these forests and imagine that you've travelled back many thousands of years to a time before humans had first appeared on the scene. It takes a few moments of quiet reflection to fully appreciate the experience but I find it has a powerful, mind-calming effect. Why is this? Without delving too deeply into the underlying philosophy, I think it's because an interest in wildlife offers an element of escape from a world increasingly dominated by humans.* It's a way of reconnecting with aspects of the old ways of life that our brains are so well adapted to, and provides a welcome break from modern, high-paced living. The more fully immersive the experience, the more effective the therapy.

Is such an experience possible in Britain in the early twenty-first century? Well, it's certainly far more difficult to achieve here but I'd say that it *is* possible, provided you are willing to relax the rules a little and have luck on your side.

It's true that we no longer have any wholly natural habitats in Britain; humans have altered them all in some way. Areas of unspoilt wilderness, together with some of the animals that once made use of them, have been consigned to history. This is not always apparent unless you have a bit of knowledge of natural history and ecology. A woodland may feel 'natural' even though it has been planted and carefully managed by generations of humans. Our upland moors, with their swathes of purple-flowered heather in late summer, also seem natural and offer a landscape that is widely appreciated. But moors only look like this because they are kept open and free of trees through grazing and burning. Vegetation that should, naturally, extend from ground level, up over our heads and towards the sky has been reduced to a thin smear of stunted heather a few centimetres high, or a short, uniform sward of grass. The great American ecologist Aldo Leopold was aware of the problem as far back as the 1940s:

---

* I explore this more fully in: Carter, I. (2021) *Human, Nature*, pp. 157–62.

One of the penalties of an ecological education is that one lives alone in a world of wounds. Much of the damage inflicted on land is quite invisible to laymen. An ecologist must either harden his shell and make believe that the consequences of science are none of his business, or he must be the doctor who sees the marks of death in a community that believes itself well and does not want to be told otherwise.*

Mountains and hill country in Britain can certainly offer remoteness from other people and a lack of artificial structures. On some days that might be enough. But in these places Aldo Leopold's words are written into the landscape itself. Platoons of sheep, cattle or deer (at unnaturally high densities due to a lack of predators) roam the hillsides, keeping the vegetation in check. George Monbiot famously referred to such areas as 'sheep-wrecked', a phrase that won him few friends in the farming community but which neatly encapsulates the extent to which the natural vegetation is suppressed by overgrazing.† There are places in the hills where landowners are trying hard to bring back the scrub and the trees, and to restore some 'wildness' and biodiversity – but, for now, if you wish to escape from the influence of humans (and our animals) it's often best to head to lower ground.

---

* Leopold, A. (1949) *A Sand County Almanac, and Sketches Here and There*. Oxford University Press, New York.
† Monbiot, G. (2013) *Feral: Rewilding the Land, Sea and Human Life*. Penguin Books, London.

One good option is to seek out a rugged stretch of coastline, taking care to avoid the most heavily used spots where holiday-makers gather. Along much of the coast of Devon there is a well-used footpath and you'll have to dodge people and those mysterious black bags full of dog turds. But there will be places where you can step away from the path and take a tangent down towards the shore. Then, it's usually not too difficult to find somewhere with a view that is nothing more than the surrounding cliffs, the beach below, flower-rich coastal grasslands and the open sea. If you're up for a bit of scrambling over rough, steep terrain then your chances of success improve, especially where livestock graze the coastal grassland. You might be able to reach a place they rarely venture and the natural vegetation has had more of a chance to flourish. The heavily trodden footpath may not be far above you but soon it all but disappears from consciousness. Whether you can avoid all signs of humanity will depend on luck and the vista out to sea. Even in remote locations, a fishing boat might come chugging into view. Or your eyes might snag on luminous pink and orange buoys, marking out lobster pots on the seabed far below.

Away from the coast, woodland is probably the best option for escaping from humans, with its enveloping shield of trees and pared-down sightlines. There are small ancient woods close to home where I can find genuine pockets of wildness, if not true wilderness. They have a high canopy of mature Beech, Ash, Wild Cherry and oaks, along with a tangled understorey including Hazel, sallows and birches. In some of these woods there is no footpath, no signs of recent management and, almost always, no other people. They appear almost abandoned in the landscape and, indeed, woodland ecologists might refer to them as 'neglected'. Such places would, at one time, have been managed for fuel and fencing materials, as were almost all our woodlands. But, for now, they stand idle and silent, all changes within them driven by natural processes.

Earlier today, to try to clear my mind, I took myself off to the nearest local wood. I walked into the middle and sat quietly, back against one of the mature oaks. It was peaceful, with no noise from motor vehicles. I tried the same mind game that works so well in the remote, wild national parks of North America, imagining this place before humans. I could hear Blackbirds, Robins, Wrens and Chaffinches singing, as they have probably done on much the same spot, uninterrupted, for thousands of years. And as Edward Thomas put it: 'Beautiful as the notes are for their quality and order, it is their inhumanity that gives them their utmost fascination, the mysterious sense which they bear to us that the earth is something more than a human estate.'* These birds would sing, as they have long sung, whether we were here or not. True, there was little chance of a Bear or Wolf or Moose ambling by, and I knew if I strolled a few hundred metres in any direction I'd soon be back at the fence line and the managed fields beyond. Humanity is not easy to escape; but sometimes there is no choice but to make the best of the limited options available. A neglected wood can help with that.

Whichever habitat you select, there is a final problem to overcome, one that is, sadly, often insurmountable. You may not

---

* I came across this quote in Lovatt, S. (2021) *Birdsong in a Time of Silence*. Particular Books, Dublin.

be able to *see* any obvious signs of human activity, but what about noise? As well as the welcome sounds made by wild animals, known as *biophony*, and other natural sounds such as the wind in the trees or a stream flowing over its gravel bed (*geophony*), we now have to contend with *anthrophony*, the multifarious noises made by humans.* These sounds are not so welcome, especially if they represent the very thing from which you are trying to get away. In the most heavily developed parts of our country the noise from roads is all pervasive. And if you do manage to find a place away from terrestrial traffic, you'll still have to contend with the air traffic above you. Here, in the sparsely populated landscapes of mid-Devon, busy roads are few and far between. And the vast jumbos that lumber across the skies do so at great height, with long gaps between them. It is still just possible to escape, at least for a short time. It's the best I can hope for. And today, as on most days, it is enough.

---

* Howard, B. S. (2019) *Dancing with Bees: A Journey Back to Nature*. Chelsea Green Publishing, London.

WILD NIGHTS OUT

If you struggle to find places with a wild feel to them during the day, waiting for a few hours might help. As darkness descends, visible signs of human activity start to diminish, and the noise made by people and their machines falls away. People retreat to their homes, traffic levels drop and the countryside becomes a quieter place. Wildlife now has a less cluttered canvas upon which to work.

I've long been drawn to that magical period when day slowly turns to night, and the select group of species that come alive with the transition. Mostly these are nocturnal animals that get tempted out before it's fully dark. Badgers often emerge from their sett when it is still light enough to watch them. Foxes are regularly encountered late in the day as the light begins to fade. And Barn Owls head out on their first foraging flights well before dusk, especially if they have young to feed. Even those true night-time specialists, the bats, venture out before it is fully dark. The large and impressive Noctule is usually the earliest to appear. It can be seen high up, using the same airspace as the Swifts – a brief merging of creatures from different realms.

In summer, patterns of birdsong track the slow change from day to night. I often listen in for an hour or so when waiting for the local Badgers to appear above ground. When I first sit down, back against a tree, most of the common woodland birds will be in full voice; taking a final opportunity to state ownership of their territory, they proclaim a warning to rivals that they are still around, before they settle down for the night. There's a rookery not far from one of the setts I watch and late evening is a time when the Rooks, and their inseparable bedfellows, the Jackdaws, swirl overhead in the direction of their nests amid a final clamouring of deep caws and excitable 'kyacks'. Then, one by one the bird sounds drop out, usually in roughly the same sequence. It's a gradual process, barely noticeable at first. But before long the wood is quieter and only the odd Blackbird, Robin and Song Thrush is still singing. If I become distracted, perhaps on that rare day when the Badgers emerge in good time, the dimming of the birdsong goes unnoticed. The first of the night's Tawny Owls makes itself heard. And when the hooting stops, suddenly there is silence.

Spending time in a place when it's fully dark is fundamentally different to being there in daylight. This goes beyond the obvious reduced visibility. The whole experience feels unfamiliar. It's as if you are not quite your normal self, with your usual mindset. I'm now in my fifties but I can still feel strangely unsettled, even frightened, when out walking in a completely dark landscape. Sometimes the fear is triggered by an unexpected shock to the system, such as a Pheasant exploding noisily from its roost. Another non-native, the tiny Muntjac Deer, is even more startling. When disturbed in woodland at night, Muntjac leap away and emit an air-shredding, screaming bark. In the middle of a wood, in the pitch blackness, it takes a few moments to recover your composure. Even then, your senses remain heightened, tuned in to the rustling of leaves and the breaking of small twigs. It is certainly easier to feel mindfully 'in the moment' on a night-time walk, all systems straining to extract as much information as possible from the surroundings.

To lessen these fears, I attempt to think logically about them. I tell myself that such a reaction is nothing more than a natural quirk of evolution, because we once walked in places where there was a high risk of ambush by unseen predators. But instinct trumps logic, especially once the sun has set. Our inbuilt responses to darkness are impossible to shake. They travel with us – a reminder of where we have come from and what we really are: for most of our existence it has been better to be wrongly scared a thousand times than to risk ignoring the approach of a predator just once.

There are a few things you can do to help make things easier on a night walk. One is to dispense with all forms of artificial light as soon as you get outside. So, no torches or smartphone screens. This helps the eyes to adjust (and stay adjusted) to low light levels, so that they can perceive as much detail as possible. It takes a surprisingly long time for this to happen, as much as 20–30 minutes for the full adjustment, and even brief doses of artificial light set the process back. Such a time-lag feels frustrating when you are dazzled by an oncoming car and have to start from scratch, or if you step out into the night from a brightly lit home. But it is another evolved adaptation. Before artificial lighting, the human eye was perfectly suited to the slow transition between day and night that our ancestors would have been familiar with. Once again, this is a small reminder of our history.

Walking across private land runs the risk of unwanted confrontation, though no doubt less so than in Stephen Graham's day when small armies of gamekeepers patrolled the ground. I don't take my mobile – a phone would make it too easy to bail out and change the plan should I run into difficulties. Without one, the only option is to keep going and make the meeting point on time, come hell, high-water or irascible landowners. The nineteenth-century rural poet John Clare was an enthusiastic explorer of his local countryside in east Northamptonshire, and was intimately familiar with it. Yet he too was wary of local landowners when he strayed from public rights of way:

> I dreaded walking where there was no path
> And pressed with cautious tread the meadow swath
> And always turned to look with wary eye
> And always feared the owner coming by;
> Yet everything about where I had gone
> Appeared so beautiful I ventured on*

My one concession to minimising the chance of unpleasantness is to pick an area with plenty of woodland. This has a twofold advantage: such places are often rich in wildlife, and they are easier to move through unnoticed than more open landscapes.

Today is Monday 21 December, the shortest day of the year, and I'm marking it by trying out a new route. A walk on this day has become a personal tradition and, as with all traditions,

---

* Clare, J. [1793–1864] 'Trespass', from *John Clare: Poems Selected by Paul Farley* (2007). Faber and Faber, London.

it gains a little more traction and power with each repetition. I have just over six miles of crow-flight to cover, but it will be longer in terms of distance travelled on foot. I'll have to cross one small lane at about halfway, but much of the route can be covered using sinuous strips of woodland that hug the valley bottom. There are no footpaths; this is not a problem within woodland, but will make it more difficult to traverse the one section that has exposed, open fields. From the map these fields appear be overlooked by farmhouses, but I'm hoping the typical high Devon hedge-banks will facilitate safe passage.

Hazel has dropped me at the edge of a wood near South Molton, an unprepossessing market town that sits just outside the National Park, with signs offering it up hopefully as the 'gateway to Exmoor'. I have five hours to make the rendezvous, and already things have started to go wrong. It's raining, of course, and I've forgotten my glasses. Anything closer than four feet away is fuzzy. My 1:50,000 Ordnance Survey map is a meaningless mass of blurred lines and shapes. Thankfully, I have a workaround: inverted binoculars allow me to peer down and resolve the lanes, woods and field boundaries, albeit only about one square kilometre at a time. This is far from ideal for route planning.

I dive into the trees and instantly feel more relaxed under cover. It's a deciduous wood with Ash, oaks, birches and a few huge Beeches towering above an understorey of Hazel and Holly. The trees are bare; most of last year's leaves are already on the ground, beginning their slow transition to soil. And it's very quiet. There is no birdsong. I find I'm more conscious of my progress than I would be in spring or summer. Perhaps it's because the sightlines are longer and so I might be noticed from further away. Or is it because, in winter, there are fewer distractions from the noises made by other creatures? I'm acutely aware of every sound I make as twigs snap beneath my boots. I catch myself looking down to try to avoid them and then, if unsuccessful, quickly turning my head to see if anyone (or anything?) has noticed. Deathly silence; skeletal trees; the bones of a landscape; rot and decay all around.

Today, darkness will descend more quickly than on any other day of the year. There is a strange sense of time passing that is at its most powerful in a midwinter wood. Here are trees that have been rooted to the same spot for perhaps a century or more; some will have been here for decades before I even existed. While this year's leaves are disintegrating around me, those for next year have already been made. They are there above my head in their millions, coiled tightly within buds, patiently waiting for their one and only chance in the sun. If I return in spring they will be present, visibly, as new leaves. Six month later and they too will be lying on the ground, slowly turning to soil. For now, all they can offer is potential – the coming spring in waiting, but not yet fully realised. On a day when nothing much is happening, these woods stand for change, and for the passage of time; they reveal the way that the years, and then the decades, rush past us almost unnoticed.

I walk on, passing through a group of old, twisted Holly trees, the view ahead now blocked by evergreen leaves, dotted with red berries. As I round the final tree, I startle a Woodcock just a few feet ahead of me. And in the same instant, *it* startles *me*, lifting sharply with an audible clatter of wings. It's loud enough that I mistake it for a Pheasant for a split second, until the shape becomes clear. The Woodcock is a plump, almost dumpy, brown bird, with short, rounded wings, and yet its escape flights have both speed and agility, making the species highly prised as a sporting bird. It is in the wader family, though atypical in shunning water in favour of damp woodlands and meadows. The Woodcock's main requirement is for ground soft enough to probe with its long, flexy-tipped bill, and cover in which to hide. In these wet woods it has plenty of both.

Further on I flush two more singles, and then two together. These individuals rise at a distance, in apparent silence. The birds think, wrongly as usual, that their cover has been blown and away they go to find another hiding place; dark shapes weaving through an obstacle course of trunks and branches – a string of inevitable collisions each, somehow, avoided at the last moment, as they seek a new spot in which to see out the day. As always when I flush a few in quick succession I begin to search for them on the ground ahead. And, as always, I'm unsuccessful. The Woodcock seems almost not to exist as a terrestrial bird. It spends virtually its entire life on the ground but it wears a cloak of leaf-litter; its intricately patterned brown, grey and black feathers are a perfect match for the woodland floor. So, for us, this is a bird of the air, glimpsed for a few seconds on the rare occasions when we stray too close and force a reveal. Only as the light fades at the end of each day will this bird launch into the air voluntarily, making for its night-time feeding sites, often transitioning from the cover of woodland out to the open fields beyond. For obvious reasons, Woodcock tend to shun busy places when hiding out during the day. Sticking to well-used paths and places busy with people is not the way to catch up with this most enigmatic and mysterious of birds.

Despite the lack of a path, it's not too difficult to pick a way through these woods, though there are no straight lines. There are fallen trunks to work around, the odd stream (heavy with recent rain) to jump, and both steep ground and waterlogged, boggy areas to negotiate. I think I'm heading in the right direction but as I've never been here before I can't be sure. For most of the day I can see no houses, farms or other evidence of people, and I have no idea how far away these things are. Perhaps there are no humans for miles in all directions. This dearth of information only adds to the experience. It brings a sense of freedom, of not knowing what is around the next corner, and an alertness that comes with trying to pick out a passable route ahead. This is not the usual way of things. Most of the time we follow signs and paths, often on visits to well-run, carefully managed nature reserves. We revisit familiar places time and time again. This too brings its benefits: we most readily notice the unusual and the way that the seasons change in places we know well. But spending time in a place we don't know is life affirming. And, for most of us, the experience it is all too rare.

As ever, I attempt to light on somewhere to eat lunch where there are no visible signs of humanity. Is this becoming a minor obsession? Walking further inside the wood I find a place that seems to fit the bill. I'm surrounded by mature trees and even with the paucity of leaves, the fields beyond are no longer visible.

All I can see are the trees and shrubs that make up a native English woodland – one that must have existed here, on this very spot, before humans first arrived in the area. If there are any distant anthropogenic sounds that might otherwise be heard, they are masked by the light breeze through the branches above.

I've already poured out a coffee when I see the problem. A single pixel of the scene has been misplaced. Hugging the trunk of an old Ash tree a few metres away is a thick stem of Ivy. It's a full five inches in diameter, one of the oldest I've seen. And there, about three feet from the ground, is a small gap where a section has been cut out by chainsaw. I can see it lying in the leaf-litter below. This is a sight that is all too familiar along the local lanes and footpaths. There must be a secret network of individuals who roam the countryside, seeking retribution for the way this plant clambers over trees to access the light. Here, in the middle of the wood, it managed to evade detection for decades judging by its size, until humans finally tracked it down. Ironically, the tree is succumbing to Ash dieback disease (as are many in this wood), so now both tree and Ivy are dying. My obsession is confirmed: I shift to a new spot where the vandalism is safely out of view.

Twenty minutes later and I'm almost standing on the lane before I realise it's there. It is sunken well beneath its flanking hedge-banks, hidden from view, with no traffic noise to give the game away. Surprisingly, Devon has more miles of road than any other county in England – it's just that most of them are tiny lanes that see very little use. The entire valley at this point is hidden from the rest of the landscape, with just a couple of old farmhouses on the upslope a few hundred metres away. I'm reminded of the thoughts of Ted Hughes when he first moved to Devon (just a few miles from where I am now) in the early 1970s:

> Buried in their deep valleys, in undatable cob-walled farms hidden not only from the rest of England but even from each other, connected by the inexplicable, Devonshire, high-banked, deep-cut lanes that are more like a defence-maze of burrows, these old Devonians lived in a time of their own.*

This quiet, concealed valley still feels timeless and somehow disconnected from the rest of the world. Alone here, and reliant on nothing but foot-power to find my way out, the effect is all the more powerful. There are no sounds, no people, and even the livestock are missing – no doubt holed up in a large shed somewhere to spare the saturated ground. In three hours of walking I've yet to encounter another human, and discounting the odd passenger jet high overhead, there has been no sound of human activity.

Nonetheless, this landscape is now very different from the one that Hughes would have known. The sense of timelessness is mere illusion, as it was in his day. In fact, he was all too aware of the pace of change as he lived and farmed here in the 1970s. He lamented the passing of the old ways in his writing, with progress driven on by 'the regular sales blast of the *Farmer's Weekly*, with its dazing propaganda for new chemicals, new

---

* Hughes, T. (1979) *Moortown Diary*. Faber and Faber, London.

methods, different chemicals, new gimmicks, new shortcuts, every possible way of wringing that critical extra per cent out of the acreage and the animals'. Fifty years on and the fields have been improved, fertilised, ploughed and reseeded beyond recognition. Apart from a few forgotten damp corners, they have lost their wild flowers and their birds, being grazed hard in summer or subject to multiple cuts of silage. The old hedges and woods still hold life, and probably look much as they did five decades ago, but few creatures can now scratch a living in the pastures that dominate the scene around me.

To reach the next section of woodland I skirt the field edges, hidden from old Devonians in their farms above by the high, thick hedges. I find a well-worn animal run in the bank and scramble up inside the hedge. Now I can work my way along the top of the wide bank, old tree stems on each side, last cut many years ago. Red Deer hooves have pushed sharp slots into the earth, showing that they too use this place to pass unseen through the landscape.

In one of the larger fields, I can just make out the lines where lost hedges once divided the land. They show as slight depressions in the ground, left from the old ditches – ghosts of an ancient landscape. What would have been four or five small fields is now a single vast expanse of grass, dominated by one or two species; there is more space for livestock and machinery but less for the wildlife that tries to cling on around the fringes.

It's a relief when I reach the next wood and slip inside, knowing that the rest of the walk will be under cover, provided I can find my way to the far end. A lone (planted?) Wych Elm near the stream still has a few luminous yellow leaves, the others lying on the ground beneath. They are by far the brightest things on view on a day that has remained stoically dull and grey. As I learn later, when I look it up, they are the largest leaves of any native tree in Britain, and I can't help wondering if they turn a brighter yellow than any other tree too. The stream carves a route through the wood. It provides an easy course to follow and will take me near my meeting point if I can stick with it for the next two miles or so.

At the edge of the wood, close to the agreed pick-up point, I have a little spare time to reflect before my lift arrives. It's been almost five hours, and apart from crossing a lane, I've been away from legitimate rights of way all this time. Does the pleasure of doing this come simply from stubbornness and the desire to break rules for the sake of it? It's more than that, I'm sure, but I find it hard to pin down.

Later that evening I re-read some sections of Nick Hayes's powerful book on trespass and the battle between private land ownership and public access.* Here, he is describing his feelings after an unexpected close encounter with Red Deer in the heart of a Suffolk wood:

> This kind of moment is only available off the path. It is an accident, unwilled and unplanned, but it comes dressed as poetry. It is prosaic, but it feels like a miracle, it feels meaningful, and it leaves me with my heart thumping in my throat. The deer were so close they felt dangerous; not

---

* Hayes, N. (2020) *The Book of Trespass: Crossing the Lines that Divide Us*. Bloomsbury, London.

aggressive, but wild-eyed and unpredictable. I would swap
a hundred nice walks along a pretty Right of Way for this
one moment of magic.

That's it. The perfect encapsulation of the joy of properly exploring
a place on your own terms rather than following a route that
has been predetermined. We spend most of our lives moving
along paths, streets and walkways that have been laid out for us
and which constrain the routes we take. We follow lines that
bind us to the will of others, surrendering any sense of freedom.
Take the path and you might see deer (though it's less likely)
but that's not the point. An encounter won't leave your heart
thumping in your chest as you stumble unexpectedly into them,
or they into you. Only off the path, much as with the Woodcock
from earlier today, will the meeting come dressed as poetry.

CONNECTIONS

TRAGEDY ON THE COMMON

Animal welfare is a contentious issue and most of us rightly strive to make sure that animals under our control are treated well. We can do rather less about the welfare of wild animals, yet there is no avoiding the fact that wildlife faces a constant battle to survive. Disease, starvation, injuries and death are routine, everyday occurrences in the countryside around us. They are integral to the way that natural systems work.

Modern humans (and our companion animals) alone are shielded from the hardships that underpin natural selection – the daily battle for survival that has influenced our species' evolution for all but a tiny fraction of its history. Most of us, in developed nations at least, no longer struggle to find food or shelter, and we don't need to worry about keeping warm or dodging predators. This is in stark contrast to the way things once were and the way they still are for the wildlife that lives around us.

Luckily for the more sensitive of human observers, much of the quest for survival happens away from our prying eyes. Animals that are cold, or hungry, or sick, or injured know to keep out of sight as best they can. They don't want to make it any easier for a predator to track them down when they are at their most vulnerable. But there is one animal in this area for which the battle for life is all too obvious.

The first sign of what's to come is the appearance of mysterious blobs of greyish-white jelly, scattered about on our local common in the middle of winter. This substance has perplexed people for generations. It's sometimes known as 'star jelly' or, less salubriously, 'star snot'. Its sudden appearance out in the open fields and on the moors, with no clues as to its origin, led people to think it must have fallen from the heavens. Where else could it have come from?

Wait a few weeks and the answer becomes obvious. From as early as the first week in January, clumps of this odd jelly start to appear in shallow water on the common and in the surrounding fields, this time in more familiar form, dotted with dozens of tiny black eggs. Star jelly is simply the remains of predated female Common Frogs that emerge from hibernation early. Individuals unlucky enough to be found out in the open, by a corvid or Heron perhaps, disappear into the food chain, leaving only the indigestible gelatinous masses that would have protected and nourished the eggs.

Once the breeding season is underway, clumps of spawn can turn up almost anywhere with water a few inches deep. There are a few small, rain-fed ponds locally but most of the spawn is deposited in diminutive, short-lived pools. In pasture fields, gateways are a favoured site, where poaching by cattle and farm machinery has created shallow depressions that fill with water. Out on the common, rain-filled wheel-ruts are used, left by the commoners when they have driven across to check on their cattle. Strangely, the Frogs themselves are rarely in evidence, especially away from the permanent ponds. Presumably all the action happens under cover of darkness, when there are fewer predators to disrupt proceedings.

By March, clumps of jelly have been replaced by living streams of tiny, black tadpoles. This is when the real trouble starts. Over the next few months, there is tadpole Armageddon. The losses are immense. As farming activities increase in the early spring, the same vehicles that helped create water-filled ruts return to exact a terrible reckoning. They follow their old tracks across the common and churn tadpoles into the mud. For any survivors, the main enemy in the coming weeks is warm, dry weather. If there is no rain for a while then the pools begin to dry out, a little more each day, and the tadpoles become restricted to ever smaller puddles. I've seen remnant pools that are essentially more tadpole than water, full of writhing animals that were once able to swim around in a far bigger area. Rain can still save them at this stage, but if it fails for a few more days, they are doomed: a lost generation reduced to a thin, rubbery film on the surface of the mud.

This, I suspect, is the reason that some Frogs risk everything by emerging from hibernation as early as possible. The cold conditions are far from ideal, and they stand out as an attractive target for predators at a time when other prey is scarce. But the earlier the eggs are produced, the better the chance that tadpoles will become froglets, able to leave the water before the early summer sun burns it all away.

The adult Frogs are caught between two options that appear equally unappealing: risk your life by emerging early to give your kids a better chance; or play a longer game, minimise the chance of predation, and hope that spawn laid later in the season occupies that is causing us to think carefully about where the limits of our responsibilities lie.

Rewilding is a controversial and ill-defined concept. Broadly though, it applies to conservation projects where natural processes are given more of a free rein. Rather than managing a habitat to achieve a particular outcome, such as maintaining heathland by clearing scrub, the approach is more flexible. The end result is determined by letting nature take its course and waiting to see what happens, more than by our own preconceived ideas. A well-known, much publicised, example from the Netherlands has highlighted one challenging issue that straddles the boundary between non-intervention and animal welfare.

The Oostvaardersplassen is an area of fifty-six square kilometres of coastal wetland set aside specifically for wildlife since the 1970s, with minimal human intervention. Early in the project, grazing animals were reintroduced to increase the chances that a variety of habitats would develop and be maintained naturally, rather than the whole site becoming dominated by uniform, unchecked scrub and trees. These included wild species such as Red Deer as well as old breeds of cattle and ponies as surrogates for the native wild horses and cattle that have long been extinct.

This project has been a huge success in terms of the wildlife that now thrives there within a diverse and dynamic range of wetland habitats that are changing all the time. Thousands of waders, ducks and geese are present in winter and there is a wide variety of breeding birds. Bearded Tits and Marsh Harriers have moved into the reedbeds, and in areas where bushes provide cover, Penduline Tits and Bluethroats can be found. Where more mature trees have grown up there are Goshawks, Willow Tits, Lesser Spotted Woodpeckers and Hawfinches.

White-tailed Eagles and Ravens also breed, taking advantage of the wide open spaces and an abundance of animal carrion. And therein lies the problem. Left unmanaged and with no natural predators, the deer, horses and cattle increased when conditions were good but starved to death in large numbers during prolonged hard winters – delighting the eagles and corvids but not the human visitors. Those running the project were reluctant to intervene because the whole idea was to let natural processes unfold. Others were not convinced, believing that the welfare of the animals should come first. In some ways, this is a larger-scale version of the Sparrowhawk–Woodpigeon conundrum that we all face occasionally. Leave things to nature or intervene on welfare grounds?

Ultimately, a compromise was reached at Oostvaardersplassen and there is now a cap on the herbivore populations with humane culling if numbers build up too much. It has been accepted that because the animals are fenced in (though the area available to them is a large one) and have no natural predators, humans retain some responsibility for their welfare. In effect, the argument hinges on the way we define 'wildlife' and 'natural' processes. Those involved hope to move further towards a fully natural situation in future at Oostvaardersplassen. Some of the fences may come down in order to reconnect the area to the rest of the landscape, including other wild areas. It is also possible that top predators such as Wolves and Lynx might recolonise (or be reintroduced) and help to naturally constrain the herbivore populations.

The aspiration remains for Oostvaardersplassen to be a place where nature dances to its own tune, as much as possible, rather than being driven by the ideas and ethical concerns of humans. Hopefully we will start to see more of this type of project in Britain in the coming years, both in the wilder and less heavily populated uplands, as well as in the lowlands. One thing is certain: the heated debates about the precise meaning of 'rewilding' and the balancing of natural processes with concerns about animal welfare and the need for interventions are sure to continue.

FLEEING HUMANITY

A mid-January walk across Rackenford and Knowstone Moor, a Devon Wildlife Trust reserve local to us, and the only large area of rough, unimproved grassland left around here. It's a wide, open expanse of nature, with views in all directions. And a good place to think. Today the early morning air is still, and cold enough for frost. Waterlogged areas crunch underfoot and the low mounds of sphagnum moss are white and stiff with ice.

After a few minutes, a question creeps up on me. I'm mildly irritated by it because it's such a simple thing and yet I've not really thought about it before, at least not in detail. A clear answer is not immediately forthcoming.

I blame the local Snipe. I often flush a few when walking here in winter, sometimes as many as 30 or 40, flying up in singles and small groups. The question I'm now pondering, having disturbed a lone bird, is why they – like most other species – flee so emphatically away from us when we venture too close.

Today, as on every visit, most Snipe break cover when I'm more than twenty metres away, often from places where they are well concealed and would no doubt have remained so. They choose not to stay hidden, or even to put just a little more distance between themselves and me. Instead, they tower up into the air at speed, firing off disgruntled, grating calls, before heading away into the distance. The noise reminds me of the squelch of a boot pulled free from thick mud, entirely appropriate for a bird leaving waterlogged ground for the air above. On misty days it's easy to lose sight of these birds as they carve zig-zagging lines across the sky, before eventually choosing a new spot to settle. I always feel a little guilty and hope they manage to find somewhere at least as secure and food rich as the place they have just abandoned.

Why do they do this? Such a rapid and energetic flight over such a long distance uses up valuable resources. And it takes them away from a place they have presumably chosen because it's where they want to be. It seems like a massive overreaction, out of all proportion with the nature of the threat; I feel almost insulted.

The smaller Jack Snipe is a bird I also see regularly, if far less often, up here on the moor. I'd guess I flush one for every thirty or so Snipe. This smaller species is far more easy-going when it comes to human disturbance, showing that other strategies are possible. They fly up only if I get to within a few metres. Sometimes they leave it so late that I almost tread on them. This laid-back approach extends to their escape flights too. They fly up, take a few seconds to pick another spot nearby, and flop down into it. No fuss, no calls of annoyance, little energy wasted. A far more rational and proportionate response – or so it seems from a human perspective.

If there's an explanation for the larger Snipe's approach then I struggle to put my finger on it. I wonder whether it's because of hunting by humans. Snipe is a quarry species, meaning that

it can legally be killed in the open season. Fly up too late and
you might become an easier target for the shotgun. Fly only a
short distance and there's a risk you will be flushed by the hunter
a second time. Perhaps, then, hunting has honed their response
and the seemingly exaggerated behaviour makes sense after all.

For a while I'm satisfied with the explanation. I pause at my
usual vantage point where I can see the edge of Exmoor, a few
miles to the north, and the dark, brooding mass of Dartmoor
away to the south – all detail erased by distance and a thin veil
of mist.

Up ahead is an area favoured by the Exmoor ponies, conservation grazers par excellence. The closely cropped sward here
offers welcome respite from the huge tussocks of Purple
Moor-grass that cover much of the site. Their long tufts of
pale-straw stems remain through the winter, and the dense
tussocks with deep troughs between are tricky to walk through
while remaining vertical. I disturb a group of Red Deer which
move from the short grass into the tussocks, all but the top of
the animals being swallowed up by the tall foliage. There is an
impressive stag and three hinds. As always, I'm amazed how
rapidly and gracefully they travel across such difficult, uneven
ground. The stag is so light on his feet, despite his heft, that his
antlers seem almost to float above the vegetation, as if bobbing
away from me on a gentle current.

And this time it's Redwings and Fieldfares, rather than Snipe,
that take my thoughts back to disturbance. I count over 100
Fieldfares, a few Redwings among them, plus several hundred
Starlings, as always packed more tightly together than the
thrushes as they frantically probe the short turf for food.

help but wonder how many more times I have left. Twenty, or thirty perhaps, if I'm lucky. That doesn't sound many.

The woods in March are brimming with promise for the summer ahead that I know from experience will never quite be fulfilled. True, the days will lengthen, the weather will warm up, the trees will ring with birdsong as the summer migrants pour in, and the vegetation will continue to unfold and fill out. But the magic of spring will not be overtopped. Much like anything good in life, the real joy is in the beginnings and in the anticipation of what is to come.

GREEN UNPLEASANT LAND

I hope this book is broadly positive in describing the pleasure that comes from noticing and interacting with wildlife. This chapter is a little different. It's not so upbeat, and it rather goes against the idea that the countryside is always a beneficial, restorative kind of place. If you are not a fan of country sports, and if you are not in the mood to read about the harsher realities of this facet of rural life, then by all means skip ahead.

If you spend a lot of time in the countryside, and especially if you enjoy exploring off the beaten track, away from well-managed nature reserves, you'll stumble upon a different kind of interaction between humans and wildlife from time to time. Whether you regard this as unpleasant will depend on your philosophy. Perhaps you are a supporter of country sports. I do try hard to keep an open mind, but I'm not a big fan and certainly not a participant. I'd rather not get too close to the action. Sometimes, though, avoidance is not an option. Even when you are minding your own business at home, sometimes the action comes to you. That's where I'll start.

A few years ago, in late summer, the new day started with the sound of gunfire. As I lay in bed and my senses gradually sharpened, I decided it must be a shotgun. Intermittent explosions, with either one shot or two in quick succession, and then a gap. Two shots indicated that the target had been missed first time and the second barrel was required. The gap was for reloading and waiting for another target to appear within range.

Our home at the time was an isolated farmhouse in the Cambridgeshire Fens, surrounded by arable land. The field on the far side of a channel of water running past the house had been growing oilseed rape until the recent harvest. Now it was a wide expanse of stubble. Most of the pods of tiny, jet-black seeds had been carted away in trailers, but some remained in the stubble, and they had not gone unnoticed. Rapeseed is an oil-rich food, favoured by many farmland birds. And today, the birds were eager to take advantage of this short-lived abundance.

The lone shooter had concealed himself in a small cloth hide near the field edge. Over his head, Woodpigeons were passing across – flying out from their overnight roost in search of food, eyes optimistically scanning the ground below. Woodpigeons are highly social birds. They move about in flocks and are drawn to feeding sites by the presence of others of their own kind; this is a signal that food is available and the location (supposedly) safe. Such behaviour is exploited by hunters. Plastic 'decoy' pigeons are set out to encourage birds flying over to drop down to feed. Judging by the number of shots ringing out, the deception had been working well.

It was mildly irritating to be woken up by gunshots, but things were about to get worse. Another shot, and then a Woodpigeon flopped down into the garden, bouncing a little on the turf. It was the first of several. The birds not killed outright carried on flying and instinctively tried to reach safety. Our garden, with its handful of mature trees, was the only cover for miles around, so that's where they headed. With their wings shattered by lead they crashed rather than landed, before flapping weakly along the ground towards the hedge – the instinct for survival intact, if not full use of their wings.

It was left to me to deal with these birds. The shooter hadn't wanted to give the game away by emerging from his hide and, in any case, he was on the other side of the water. Having dispatched the two birds I'd managed to catch by swinging their heads hard against a tree trunk (the only option I could think of), I drove around to the far side of the drain to have a word. The stubble around his hide was littered with the dead and the dying. He cleared them up as we talked, irritated that his sport had been interrupted but nevertheless all but filling his car boot with pigeons. He was unapologetic, pleading – rather hopelessly in the circumstances, I thought – that it hadn't been his intention to injure birds. There followed a mini lecture on societal expectations about cheap food and the need for effective pest control. I asked if he would eat all these birds: 'A few perhaps, but they'll mostly feed the ferrets.'

My gripe was not so much about the rights and wrongs of pigeon control. Here the pigeons were gleaning unwanted waste, but they can cause major damage to growing crops. It's just that killing wildlife is not really my thing. I didn't enjoy such close proximity to the action, and I especially disliked having to chase dying birds around my own garden in order to deliver the *coup de grâce*. I pictured the likely scene had my young children been there to see this; I could imagine their stricken faces as crippled, bloodstained wildlife started to plummet from the skies.

Much the same scenario can play out regularly if you live close to a Pheasant shoot. Simon Barnes wrote about it in his book *On The Marsh*.* He lives in rural Norfolk, and every Saturday through the shooting season he and his son Eddie are on high alert for the sound of gunfire. Their horses get distressed when shooting starts in the adjacent field. So they must be brought back to their stable, ideally before the shooting begins, to be comforted through the barrage of gunfire and the gentler thud of Pheasant on grass.

The killing of Pheasants for sport is so widespread that even if you don't live near a shoot there's a good chance of encountering the fallout when out and about in the landscape. Occasionally our Cocker Spaniel finds a wounded Pheasant on a walk, hunkering down in the hedge, able to flap limply across the ground but incapable of flight. These birds are simply waiting for death having managed to elude the retrieving dogs on shoot day. If I'm able to catch up with them, I put them out of their misery. It's the decent thing to do but, once again, it's not much fun.

Our dog also regularly locates piles of dead Pheasants dumped along the local lanes. I'd rarely noticed this phenomenon before becoming a dog owner, because the bodies are frequently well concealed by vegetation. But Teazel picks up the scent and dives into the nettles and rank grass to investigate. Countless hundreds of carcasses are dumped in this way locally, full of lead shot,

---

* Barnes, S. (2019) *On the Marsh: A Year Surrounded by Wildness and Wet*. Simon & Schuster, London.

unappealing (and unsafe) as food – nothing more than the unwanted spoils of a session of target shooting.

Shooting Woodpigeons and Pheasants is perfectly legal, although, to borrow a shooting expression, it's considered 'poor form' to shoot so close to a garden. But our old home also provided opportunities to watch illegal activities. Hare coursing is common in the Fens. I saw it dozens of times over the years and the large, open fields surrounding the house were well suited to this activity. Come the autumn, when the harvest was done and the Brown Hare became visible once again, I couldn't help but start to look out for the men with their short leads and long dogs.

Hare coursers walk the fields, their dogs under close control. If a Hare is seen the dogs are quickly slipped from their restraints and the chase begins. The enjoyment (so I'm told) is in the skill of the dogs, the competition between them, and finding out whether or not they can match the speed and agility of our fastest land mammal. Often they can. Large sums of money are apparently wagered on the outcome.

Hare coursing is taken seriously by the Cambridgeshire police rural crime team. I must have phoned them twenty times or more over the years and more often than not they sent cars to attend. Sometimes several police vehicles appeared within a few minutes, blue lights flashing, sending the criminals scrambling to recover their dogs and get back to their vehicles. I had a good vantage point from my study window upstairs and watched some spectacular car chases unfold along the local lanes and byways, and sometimes, in desperation, across the stubble fields. Twice, the police helicopter appeared overhead, adding to the drama.

On one occasion several men scattered on foot in order to avoid police as they fanned out across a field. Mirroring the wounded Woodpigeons, one ended up seeking the only cover on offer. As I came out into the garden there he was, crouched underneath the Leylandii hedge flanking our lawn, his back against our fence and his dog sat calmly next to him. Wary of repercussions, I didn't want to give him away in an obvious manner. So unseen, I walked quietly out of the gate and gesticulated at the nearest uniform, silently attracting his attention; then, almost whispering, I guided him to the spot.

Since we moved to Devon, we've seen no more hare coursing, and rather few Hares, but there is no escaping the age-old battle between dog and wild mammal. The quarry of interest in this area is red rather than brown: the Red Fox and Red Deer. The Hunting Act of 2004, in theory banning hunting with dogs, has, it seems, yet to cut through. Loopholes are exploited, but mainly, the legislation is simply ignored. Our house is only a mile or so from the Tiverton Staghounds' Kennels. When the wind is in the right direction, we can hear the baying of hounds at feeding time or when they are about to set out on a hunt. During the autumn deer rut it's possible to hear stags roaring and hounds wailing from their kennels at the same time. It makes me wonder if the deer or dogs ever make the connection as their voices float out across the fields. Judging by the apparently relaxed behaviour of the deer I've observed, it would appear not.

Fox hunting is also common locally, and casual encounters with a hunt of one kind or another are a near weekly occurrence from late summer through to the spring. The police response offers the starkest of contrasts with hare coursing. At first, I phoned them with information about illegal activity, as I'd done many times in the Fens. I soon realised I was wasting my time.

The hunts do have some support locally, especially among landowners and, more widely, among older people. But opinion is sharply divided. Based on my unscientific straw poll of local people, when the subject comes up, opposition heavily outweighs support, even in this highly rural area. Many people are horrified that it continues so long after it was banned, and more appalled still that it is almost always ignored by the police. Every so often a new video emerges of a stag being chased into someone's garden, or a Fox being swallowed up by a pack of hounds. The odd cat goes missing, livestock are spooked (or worse) and a Border Terrier cross was killed a few years ago in our nearest village. The staghounds came into the dog owner's garden, the pack mentality kicking in when the pet dog sought to defend its patch. It stood no chance, despite the best efforts of the owner to intervene. Substantial hush money, complete with non-disclosure agreement, was offered and in this case refused, so perhaps this happens more often than we might think. A court case followed but the judge dismissed it, noting, somewhat insensitively you might think, that 'dogs will be dogs'.

I have great respect for the police and the difficult job they do. I was thoroughly impressed by the way the Cambridgeshire rural crime team tried to clamp down on hare coursing. But I have a little less respect for the force than I once did. Hunting in Devon is a criminal activity that is highly organised and highly visible. It takes place frequently amid much fanfare. It is the subject of recent legislation to ban it, and is widely opposed by the public. Yet a tacit agreement seems to have been reached between hunts and police that their activities can proceed with minimal, if any, threat of enforcement. The police appear to have picked a side, happy to accept the obvious pretence that hounds are following a laid trail rather than chasing wildlife. Knock on the door of any rural house in mid-Devon and, hunt supporter or not, the occupant will be able to tell you what really happens. Good intelligence would not be hard to come by if only the will was there to gather it.

Is the difference between approaches to fox hunting and hare coursing the fact that one tends to involve wealthy, influential people and the other is more often a pastime for those at the other end of the wealth spectrum? I'd like to think that can't possibly be true. But, based on my own experiences, I struggle to see any other plausible explanation.

We have not yet had a hunt come through our garden, though that's mainly because our track has a gate and the garden is stock fenced to keep out the cows. But we've seen the huge stag hounds come lolloping across the adjacent fields several times, and once I saw a Fox run across the same field with the hounds not too far behind. That was one of the first incidents I witnessed and, full of righteous indignation, I immediately phoned the police. No cars, or helicopters, were dispatched.

Local people who love wildlife and enjoy living close to it are worn down by these illegal activities, taking place week in, week out. Their views are easy to ignore. They have no voice, or at least not one that seems to count for very much. They endure the sights and sounds of organised crime on their doorstep because there is no other choice. But the local countryside is tainted as a result, its restorative power diminished, and faith in the workings of our law enforcement bodies sorely tested.

There are other things you may come across, and wish you hadn't, if you are keen on wildlife and don't especially enjoy seeing it killed. If you stray from nature reserves and footpaths (and sometimes if you don't) you're likely to witness the varied approaches for tackling creatures deemed problematic for gamebirds, agriculture or species of conservation concern. There are snares for Foxes, tunnel traps for Stoats, and cleverly designed cages to catch Carrion Crows, Magpies and even Badgers. If you live near a grouse moor and make use of the suggestion from earlier in this book to follow a stream, you may see a trap every fifty metres or so. Logs are placed over the water to provide handy crossing points, and in the middle of each sits a trap, ensuring that Stoats and other small predators do not reach the other side.

Badgers enjoy full legal protection but exceptions are made in order to limit the spread of bovine tuberculosis to cattle. We learnt recently that our local countryside has been included in one of the cull zones that now cover large parts of the country. In these places, licences are issued allowing up to 80% of an area's Badgers to be killed, by trapping or shooting. Now, every time I walk past one of the local setts, I wonder whether it will still be active, or if I might find one of the cages used in the cull, baited with peanuts. It has deterred me from going out to watch the animals in the evening because seeing them would only add to the sense of loss if they were subsequently killed off.

I read recently about an elderly woman, living alone after the death of her husband and restricted to her home in Somerset during the height of the coronavirus pandemic. She has been feeding the local Badgers in her garden for years and has come to know many of them individually through their behaviour and distinctive facial patterns. She takes great pleasure in looking out for them each evening. Or at least that's how things were. She too lives in a cull zone and has now lost 'her' Badgers. Another human casualty of the cull – and a further diminishment of the joy and solace that wildlife can bring.

The killing of wildlife as a pastime, or because it impacts on other things, is a contentious and complex subject. I'm not saying we should necessarily stop doing it, but surely the full impacts on everyone in society must be taken into account. I often hear that because we live in a free country it's up to individuals to make up their own mind and act accordingly. And yet, in our densely populated landscapes, the choices made by individuals do not play out in isolation; they affect other people, sometimes in ways that impinge on their freedom to enjoy wildlife and time spent outdoors.

I'm reminded of an experience described by Richard Mabey, one that influenced his decision to finally speak out about the rights of non-hunters after years of staying out of the debate.*

---

* Mabey, R. (2010) *A Brush with Nature: Reflections on the Natural World*. BBC Books, London.

He was guiding a party of primary schoolchildren around a National Nature Reserve in Norfolk, only to have the day ruined when a hail of gunfire resulted in 'a lake covered with dead and wounded birds, and a group of frightened and distressed children, bewildered at what right these men had to kill birds on a nature reserve *and* take away their freedom to enjoy birds peaceably'. An experience wrecked by noise, death and wounding, with who knows what long-term consequences. Then there is the old lady in Somerset, sat alone of an evening, looking out into the stillness of her empty garden.

THE AMATEUR NATURALISTS

I've reached an age where I spend plenty of time looking back, reflecting on how things once were in comparison to how they are now. It's easy to have a rose-tinted view. Our minds snag on the negative aspects of life today, while slipping easily into nostalgia for times long gone. Countless parents have bored their kids by telling them that the world is going to pieces and things used to be much better. Perhaps the doom merchants have a point this time, or is this just the same old trick playing out, once again, as the generations run on?

There can be little doubt that wildlife is in trouble, assailed from all sides as farming become ever more intensive, semi-natural habitats are destroyed and the climate continues to warm. Endless reports and scientific assessments document losses and declines that show no sign of slowing down. In Britain we are lucky to live in a country where our wildlife is more closely monitored than almost anywhere else. And, contrastingly, we are unlucky to find ourselves in one of the most nature-depleted places on the planet. Our ancient woodlands, heathlands and flower-rich meadows have been reduced to mere fragments of what they once were; but at least we have shelves full of paper to record the losses in fine detail. As the shelves fill up, so the declines continue.

Is there any cause for optimism? Much depends on your personal outlook. One option is to travel your way to a life full of wildlife. For those with time and money (and pandemics aside), we live in a golden age. Yes, wildlife across the globe has been greatly diminished. But our ability to journey to inspiring places has never been greater. If you could choose the period to live out your life, in the hope of seeing as wide a diversity of wildlife as possible, you would do well to pick now. Any earlier and your travel options would be far more limited; any later and while travel might be easier still, wild places would no doubt have been further diminished.

If you prefer your home comforts to travel, watching wildlife documentaries on TV can plug the gap; you can immerse yourself in scenes of wilderness from around the planet and wonder what all the fuss is about.

Is a positive spin still possible here in Britain, given the scale of losses? On a good day I like to think so, in part because we have no choice but to make the best of what's left. Pockets of interesting habitat are still out there. And information about how to find them, and what you are likely to see, is easy to come by. Within a few miles of home, I can walk through places rich in wildlife: in nature reserves, on the local common, through forgotten woods, or tracing the course of a stream running through swampy field corners, fragments of habitat survive where time is well spent. So much has been lost, but there is so much yet to lose.

Alongside the changes to our countryside, there have been huge changes in the way we interact with it. In just a few generations our relationship with nature has radically altered. This reflects the diminishing opportunities to experience wild places; there are fewer of them and more of us now live in urban areas or landscapes dominated by intensive farming. There are also more competing interests these days. An innate love of engaging with wildlife is present in almost every young child. These days, as children get older, that love often fades – other interests, usually indoor pastimes, begin to take precedence. The wider world, accessible as never before through our electronic devices, is an irresistible draw for curious, ambitious young minds. A basic knowledge and understanding of the countryside and its wildlife would once have developed in nearly all children; it was a natural progression from that early, instinctive love of nature. Nowadays, that is the exception rather than the rule – most kids quickly move on to other things.

All this is brought home to me most clearly by thinking about my own experience of growing up and how it differed from that of my parents and of my own children. When I stayed indoors, especially during the long school holidays, I was bored witless; there was very little to do. But from the age of about eight I was allowed to roam freely from the house, armed only with a few simple words of advice: 'Take care when crossing the road; don't get into a stranger's car; and *don't* waste all your money in Mr Lovatt's sweet shop.' I was obliged to follow only one rule: 'Be back home in time for tea (or bed) or there'll be trouble.' There was often trouble.

We lived in a largely rural area and the fields, woods and ponds offered interesting spaces where we could climb trees and play games. Wildlife was sometimes part of the entertainment, though when I was young, I didn't venture out specifically to engage with it. It was incidental rather than sought. But if an area of rough grass was full of grasshoppers then an hour could be spent seeing who could catch the most, or the biggest. The Bracken-covered hillside near home was valued for no other reason than because it was away from adults and allowed us to construct a network of hideouts beneath the fronds. I doubt if I knew what the plant was called.

Conker-hunting was an exception. We *did* visit places specifically to collect these nuts in the autumn, and spent hours hurling sticks up into the canopy to dislodge choice-looking examples. When we managed to hit a good cluster of fruits, there would be a shower of split skins and a pulse of excitement as we scanned the leaf-litter. If we were unlucky the nuts would be 'whiteys' (not yet fully ripe), 'flaties' (not much good for conker fights) or even 'water-babies' (small, poorly formed and soft inside).

Another exception was fishing. I learnt the names for the most common fish, and places where you could catch them, though I never seemed to have much luck. The local canal produced a few Eels, which in those days were viewed as stealers of bait rather than a worthwhile catch. They were difficult to get hold of and remove from the hook, and they thrashed relentlessly, leaving trails of slime and frustration in their wake.

One horrific memory, still vivid after four decades, involved snagging my hook in a tangle of vegetation and snapping the line. I gave up in disgust and headed home. The next day, with renewed determination, I went back and waded out from the bank to retrieve it. I found the line and followed it back to where it was caught. There, on the end, was a dead Moorhen. It had tried to eat the worm on the hook. I told no-one, but it was a lesson learnt about the consequences of carelessness: our behaviour has direct impacts on the other animals living around us.

I didn't go birdwatching until my later teens; when I was younger, I didn't know the names of many birds. There was a brief phase of egg-collecting which appealed to my hunting and collecting instincts, but it ended abruptly when 'Auntie' Marjorie, from a few doors down, warned that I could be sent to prison.

When I was older, I did start to learn more about wildlife through books and the monthly magazine of the Young Ornithologists' Club. The two books that had most influence were Gerald Durrell's *The Amateur Naturalist* and the Reader's Digest *Birds of Britain.** The bird book was the one that, finally, taught me to identify the common local species. It was given to me by my Uncle David and Auntie Pam for my fifteenth birthday and I'm not sure I've ever properly thanked them. Perhaps that's because they included my unmentionable middle name in the inscription, and added 'happy spotting' for good measure – but I'm over that now, so I really must make amends.

For each species in *Birds of Britain* there was a small photo of the bird, and a map to show where you might find it. Every bird was also painted in numerous different poses, indulging in natural behaviours, so you got a real feel for how it went about its life. And the images included enough background to suggest the preferred habitat. The text focused on where birds lived and

---

* Durrell, G., with Durrell, L. (1982) *The Amateur Naturalist: A Practical Guide to the Natural World*. Hamish Hamilton, London. Various contributors (1981) *Field Guide to the Birds of Britain*. The Reader's Digest, London.

what they got up to, while the writing was colourful enough to make birds seem interesting and memorable. The Redshank demonstrates 'extreme alertness' and so is regarded as 'the sentinel of the marsh' – I've never forgotten that. The male Reed Bunting is 'reminiscent of a Victorian Guards officer'. And the short text for the humble Blackbird finds space for the words of an eighteenth-century essayist, Joseph Addison, quoted from *The Spectator*: 'I value my garden more for being full of Blackbirds than of cherries, and very frankly give them fruit for their songs.' The book is full of things like that. It was published in 1981 but seems to hark back to a lost age when this sort of knowledge was more widely known and appreciated. I'm constantly surprised it isn't mentioned more often when naturalists list their favourite childhood books.

I still thumb through *Birds of Britain* occasionally, and it provides a salutary reminder that nothing stays the same for very long. I had yet to encounter a Willow Tit when I received the book but I learnt that there were up to a hundred thousand pairs in Britain. Not anymore. The maps showed that Cirl Buntings and Red-backed Shrikes could still be chanced upon across much of southern England, and I looked out (in vain) for both. The Hobby, Goshawk and Red Kite were either scarce or absent from the English countryside, while Crane, Little Egret and Cetti's Warbler sneaked into the book as unobtainable rarities, given just a few words and a single small image. These were birds to dream about rather than look out for in the local landscape.

Gerald Durrell's book was very different. I wasn't interested in his titles on collecting and keeping exotic animals, but much of *The Amateur Naturalist* was about native British wildlife and how best to experience it for yourself. I was especially drawn to the double-page photos showing things that had been collected from the wild in each habitat. There were feathers, skulls, bits of broken eggshell, hazelnuts opened by various small mammals, as well as leaves and fungi. He was also not beyond collecting a few animal specimens to add 'life' to these pages. The text describes how creatures interact with each other, and how they survive and prosper. The book also outlines the fieldwork techniques that can be used to better understand wildlife. It gave me a basic grounding in ecology. For this book it's my parents to whom I owe the debt of gratitude.

These books changed my life. I decided to do a degree in ecology based more on Gerald Durrell's take on the subject than anything I'd learnt at school. And my main passion, and later my career, involved birds and their conservation.

My dad grew up in the small village of Hillesley, in rural Gloucestershire, during the rationing years after the Second World War. When I talk to him about his memories of childhood, I'm struck by two things. Firstly, knowledge of wildlife and the countryside was seen as a routine, everyday part of life from a young age – so much so that he struggles to say how it came to him. Not so much from books or school, he thinks, but probably more 'by osmosis, simply through spending time in the countryside and talking to other children about it'.

The other aspect that stands out is the way in which the countryside then was far more than simply a place to play and while away the hours. In those tough, postwar years it was used as a way of making life more tolerable. Moorhen nests were raided so the eggs could be eaten. Hazelnuts and sweet chestnuts were gathered and buried in a tin so they would keep until Christmas.

Animals were caught for food as well. A few of the older kids tied Woodpigeon squabs into their nest so that the adult birds continued to feed them and they could be harvested when nice and plump. Rabbits were caught with wire snares, the trick being to find a place on a Rabbit trail where a small hop was required. If the wire was set in just that spot, the animal would jump into the loop, ensuring that it was caught. Some people kept ferrets to help increase the catch. Dad recalls people walking back to the village with the 'coneys' strung out along a pole, slung over the shoulder. Mushrooms were gathered and Watercress was valued as a source of greens, to be collected only from fast-flowing streams to make sure it was safe. The local wood was owned by someone my grandfather knew well and so the family were allowed to cut stakes for the peas and beans in their vegetable plot.

There was money to be made too. Blackberries were gathered in huge quantities and sold to a man who came by the village regularly, parking his van next to the pub to conduct the trans-actions. They were sold by weight and kids would spray them with water to help nudge the price a little higher. My dad kept pigs, buying them when they were a few weeks old and fattening them up to be sold on. Acorns gathered from the woods could be used to save on expensive feed. A sign of the times was that profits were as likely to go towards new school shoes as anything more frivolous.

My mum had a more urban upbringing, living in the suburbs of London in Welling for much of her childhood. Unsurprisingly, she had far less contact with nature and remembers the nearby parks as places for fresh air and exercise rather than for engaging with wildlife. From days out in London she recalls the Feral Pigeons massing in Trafalgar Square and the Ravens at the Tower of London, noting that they held more interest than any of the dull buildings or their contents. Perhaps this hints at an interest in nature that was there but had been suppressed through lack of opportunity.

The war opened up a wider window onto the countryside. Mum was evacuated as a young girl to a coastal village near Eastbourne, East Sussex to stay with relatives. Here, there were regular fishing trips with her uncle and she remembers her delight at finding Primroses and Bluebells in the local woods, two plants that she stills holds in special affection. She would pick a few to bring back to the house – one of the simplest, yet most effective acts of connection with nature, and one that is far less common in modern times.

In contrast to my dad, she has fond memories of books, and one in particular that taught her about wildlife. Enid Blyton was popular in my childhood, but back in 1944 she published a volume called the *Nature Lover's Book*, with poems, short stories about countryside walks, and colourful, lifelike illustrations.* My mum loved it and even remembers the name of the friendly uncle who imparted his knowledge so readily in the stories:

---

* Blyton, E. (1956) *Enid Blyton's Nature Lover's Book*. Evans Brothers, London (first published 1944).

'Mr Merryfield, I think it was, though we just called him Mr Merry!' As a child myself, I can remember pulling that book down from the shelf and leafing through the pages. It looked and sounded rather formal and old fashioned, but that didn't stop me reading it.

My own children, Ali and Ben, were born either side of the new millennium. Wildlife was very much part of their early experiences, in the garden at first, and later out in the woods and fields. I phoned them today, interrupting their respective university studies to ask about their memories of early childhood. I was surprised how much detail came flooding back to them, and then to me. There were evenings peering out of the kitchen window watching Fox cubs clamber around by the climbing frame. There was the time we wrapped up warm and lay on the ground at the edge of a field to watch shooting stars. There were a few failed attempts to see Badgers and then one successful trip, remembered more for the two buck Muntjac that chased and barked at each other relentlessly in the fading light.

Visits to my parents' house, 'Eastfield', invariably involved a pond-dipping session and an accumulation of Palmate Newts in a goldfish bowl – to be shown off and then carefully returned to the water. Some of those animals must have been caught dozens of times over the years. We rescued Toads from the lane near the village pond and deployed small mammal traps overnight, catching Bank Voles, Wood Mice and the occasional Common Shrew. We left the porch light on overnight to see what moths would visit, before trying to work out which species they were before breakfast the next day. Even now if they find a moth it quickly appears on WhatsApp with an expectation (usually unfulfilled) that I'll tell them its name.

There were holidays on the south coast and then in north Cornwall, near Tintagel, where we spent hours dangling crab lines into the harbour and later fished for Mackerel. Rock-pooling was a favourite pursuit, as it was on my own childhood holidays, allowing yet more creatures to be caught and temporarily held captive. There was a spring visit to Shetland where we 'rescued' Oystercatcher chicks from the road, dodged the overprotective skuas with a mixture of delight and genuine trepidation, and watched Otters scrambling along the rocky beaches. On Unst, as far north as it's possible to go in Britain, we were entranced by Puffins waddling past our rucksacks as we ate lunch, and watched Gannets swirling around the updrafts of the immense cliffs that make up their colony.

One striking thing about all these memories is that they are shared; they are things we did together as a family. That's the most obvious difference between my children's experience and that of my own childhood: my kids had far less scope for the independent learning that was routine for previous generations. When I was growing up, if I wanted to escape from parental control and do my own thing, I wandered off into the woods and open spaces. Now that option is closed off because of fears about safety. If escapism is what children are after, they must get it by staying indoors and engaging with a virtual world, one that comes with its own concerns about safety and wellbeing.

The modern, parentally guided approach to the countryside is not all bad. When we did things as a family, we talked about what we saw and some of the problems that wildlife faces at the hands of humans. I like to think my children learnt something about the natural world as a result. They certainly got to know the names of some of our common birds and plants at an earlier age than I did. Another advantage, for me if not for them, is that we can now reminisce fondly about days spent together exploring the countryside, as indeed we have just done.

I can see a clear transition in just three short generations, one that I think will ring true for many families. For my parents, my dad especially, the countryside was integral to everyday life. All the local children knew it well, made good use of it and learnt about it from each other as well as from their parents. It was a way of life. By the time of my own childhood, some of that intimacy had gone. I count myself lucky to be in the last generation allowed to explore the outdoors more or less on my own terms. But the countryside for me was a playground and a source of entertainment. Other than a few family expeditions to pick blackberries or sweet chestnuts, my connection with the wildlife was less meaningful and my knowledge not especially deep. Only later in childhood did I become seriously interested in the natural world, and that was very much as a hobby. Tellingly, it was not something to be shared with my peers because it was seen as an unusual interest and a rather uncool one at that. My dad chatted to his friends and classmates about wildlife. I kept quiet.

Because of my own positive experiences with freedom, I had wanted a similar thing for my children. I battled against the prevailing view that unsupervised roaming was just too risky. But, in the end, I mostly went along with it. The quandary parents face is summed up by something I read recently by E. O. Wilson, one of the greatest biologists of our time. He credits unsupervised, hands-on experience in childhood as a crucial factor in his development: 'Better to be an untutored savage for a while. Better that the summer at Paradise Beach [where he honed his interest in wildlife] was not an educational exercise planned by adults. Better that it was an accident in a haphazard life.'*

During one such unsupervised session, the young Wilson hooked a sharp-spined pinfish and contrived, by pulling too hard on his fishing rod, to jerk it into his right eye. His eyeball was pierced by a spine and subsequently lost most of its function. Another fishing accident, though with a far higher personal cost than my own. And another example of an independent lesson well learnt, although this time with life-long repercussions. Perhaps this would have happened even had an adult been present, and perhaps not. Not many parents these days are willing to take the chance.

We live in a golden age for international travel and connectivity with the wider world. But the golden age when children could explore the local countryside on their own terms has gone forever.

---

* Wilson, E. O. (1994) *Naturalist*. Allen Lane, London.

WINTERING

For many people, it seems, winter is a problem, with its low light levels and plummeting temperatures. It's something to be dreaded in advance and endured when it comes. Christmas and New Year excepted, this is a time to hunker down and withdraw, until it is finished with for another year.

I've taken the chapter heading from Katherine May's poignant book on the subject. In *Wintering*, she acknowledges the challenges but also hints at a more positive aspect to the season; we should, she suggests, try to embrace it and use it to our advantage.* Partly this is about enjoying the good things that it brings, but also it is about acceptance. If cold weather and short days are not your thing then that's fine; take advantage of the chance to wind-down, rest and look forward to the better times to come.

I have sympathy for those who struggle, but I've always looked forward to winter. By the end of summer, I've grown weary of hot and humid weather with its induced lethargy, heat haze and sleepless nights. Even the woods and fields seem to have had

---

* May, K. (2020) *Wintering: The Power of Rest and Retreat in Difficult Times*. Rider, London.

enough. The leaves have lost that bright, fresh green from the early summer, and lush vegetation along the hedgerows is starting to die back and collapse to the ground. Autumn's cooler, fresher days bring relief, not to mention an influx of migrant birds, an abundance of fungi, nuts and berries, and the magic of autumn colour as the leaves turn. Now I can begin to look forward to even colder days ahead and the kind of weather that only winter brings.

As with all seasons, there are different ways to delineate winter. Most people, I think, would see November as a winter month; the first month when we can expect proper winter weather and need the appropriate clothing to cope with it. Meteorologists, too, define the seasons using the weather, but take winter to be the year's coldest three months: December, January and February. Then there is astronomical winter which runs from the solstice in late December, through to the spring equinox three months later. That also marries reasonably well with the coldest period of the year. And yet it starts on the shortest day, just at the point when light levels are beginning to increase once again – such is the time-lag between day-length and its effects on the weather.

The autumn equinox, with equal hours of light and dark, and the winter solstice in late December are significant dates. But there is another important day that I anticipate even more keenly. It is unpredictable, and despite its appeal it almost always catches me off guard. One morning, I'll venture outside to open the henhouse and notice an unexpected, refreshing coolness in the air. Looking around, there it is, once again: a thin sheen of ice, coating the grass, or sometimes just the car. It may be so precarious and fragile that sight alone is not convincing: touch is required to dispel any doubts, and I've been fooled more than once by heavy dew on a cool (but not quite cool enough) autumn morning.

This year, the first frost, or rather *my* first frost was on 4 November. As is so often the case, it was a fleeting affair, available only to early risers and soon wiped away by the rising sun. It was the return of ice last present almost six months ago, following a late and damaging frost on 12 May, well after the first Swifts had returned for the summer. My diary mournfully notes the dead, browned-off potato plants in the vegetable plot, and that some of the young leaves on our local Beech trees had gone the same way. Frost in late spring is not welcome; we've had quite enough of it by then. But frost in the autumn is a thing of beauty; it's a reacquaintance with an old friend. Much like the first warm sun of the year, shining on bare skin in March, the first frost of the winter offers a hint of what is to come. Spring sunshine is a prompt for heightened activity – a call for readiness for the longer days ahead. The opposite is true in the autumn. The frost is a sign that we might begin to relax and decompress, just a little.

I once connected my love of wintery weather with school, or rather with a day or two away from its unwanted routines and constraints. Snow brought with it the prospect of freedom. As a child, I'd avidly watch the weather forecast at the end of the news. If it was encouraging, I'd spend the evening peering through the curtains, looking hopefully up into the sky. Or I'd open them fully and put the outside light on so that any falling flakes would pass through its glow and be easy to see. On the rare evenings when it did actually snow, my obsession turned to whether or not it would settle, and whether it would be deep enough to keep the school bus safely in its depot. This didn't happen often but when it did, there was cause for wild celebration. A day stretching ahead with the twin joys of not going to school and being able to explore a landscape utterly transformed. Lying snow is already less common than it was in my childhood. Predictions suggest that it may soon be largely a thing of the past in lowland Britain as climate change begins to take effect.

If snow is becoming scarce, ice offers the next best thing. The Met Office defines 'ice days' as those where the temperature remains at, or below, freezing for 24 hours. They too are now less frequent; a mild or average winter may see none at all in low-lying areas. For that reason, I've adopted my own, somewhat modified definition, which helps add a few more to the year: I'm content that it's an 'ice day' if I can find sheltered spots where a few small pockets of ice cling on all day after an overnight frost.

A few days ago, I took the dog to the common on a promising sunny afternoon. The temperature had nudged up to around 3–4°C and the white, frosted landscape formed overnight had long gone. But in the hollows and along the north side of strips of woodland it was possible to find a few surviving traces. Even the largest tussocks of Purple Moor-grass created safe havens where the sun could not penetrate, and the grass on one side retained its white feathering of ice and its stiffness. By around three o'clock I was satisfied that the battle had been won. I could feel on my face that the temperature was dropping once again; the surviving patches of ice would be safe until the following morning at least.

The next day was colder still, barely creeping above freezing. And in the woods fringing the common I fulfilled an ambition.

After years of looking and hoping, there in front of me, resting on the leaf-litter, was a fallen branch with a white, furry coating. I picked it up and admired the tufts of 'hair' springing up, as if by magic, from within the rotting wood, each several centimetres long. A clump dropped to the ground coming to rest among the dead leaves as if it had been pulled from a passing Reindeer. This was hair ice, made up of thousands of impossibly thin, candyfloss-like strands. Its formation is dependent on the presence of a certain species of fungus within the dead wood, as well as air that is sufficiently moist and a temperature that holds close to freezing point for long enough. When all that comes together, tiny filaments of ice push out gradually from within the wood and hold their integrity as they coat the branch with fur. The required conditions are so particular that this effect is apparently mostly restricted to latitudes between 45 and 55 degrees north. When I got home, I worked out that the common sits just above 51 degrees north – close to the mid-point and the sweet spot for hair ice.

Why *does* cold weather and its associated phenomena hold such appeal now that I don't have to fret about school? Is it because snow and ice still carry some of the magic they held in childhood and take me easily back to those days? Katherine May puts it like this in *Wintering*:

> Snow vanquishes the mundane. It brings the everyday to
> a grinding halt, and delays our ability to address our dreary

responsibilities. Snow opens up the reign of the children, high on their unexpected liberty, daredevil and impervious to the cold.

It is also, I think, down to an appreciation of seasonal variation and the novelty of change. Ice and snow are welcome simply because I forget what they look and feel like after a long, hot summer. I forget how transformative a layer of snow, or even a sharp frost, can be. I need to be reminded how snow softens both the shapes and sounds of the countryside, and the strange way that it throws light up from the ground and makes the birds passing overhead look otherworldly. I forget how invigorating the cold air feels as it bites at the fingertips and numbs bare skin.

I wonder if there is even more to it than that. The impact of serious exposure to cold is not to be underestimated, but when it is controlled, could it have a beneficial effect? There is increasing interest in the health benefits of cold-water immersion. Devotees swim briefly each day in the sea, or a suitable river or lake, and evidence suggests this has a measurable effect on wellbeing.* A cold shower achieves much the same effect if you can bring yourself to step into one. And the Scandinavian obsession with sauna often involves a ritual dip in cold water or a roll in the snow to end each session.

Perhaps, then, a walk on a bitterly cold day can have similar benefits. It certainly seems that way to me, much as putting ice on an injury is thought to aid the healing process. I am refreshed coming back indoors after a walk in the cold in a way that feels

---

* This subject is explored further in Katherine May's book (see above).

different to an outing in milder conditions. Exposed flesh is glowing, even tingling if it's very cold. And there is that strange twin pleasure of being glad to be back inside in front of the fire, but also happy to have been outside and felt the full force of winter. The short days help with this. If it's dark outside I can assuage any guilt that I might otherwise have for spending too much time relaxing indoors. Indeed, part of the magic of winter is the fact that we can so easily escape its worst effects by stepping inside and away from it. Things were not always this way. A long, cold spell would once have brought misery and death for those not ready to face it. It still does the same to many of the animals we leave outside when we close the door behind us.

It took a re-reading of Bill McKibben's book *The End of Nature* to help reaffirm another small joy that cold weather brings.* As long ago as 1990 he was lamenting the fact that no wild habitat could, any longer, be considered truly 'natural'. Even in the most remote, untouched forest, the plants, trees and animals have been influenced by a warming climate for which humans alone are responsible. Day to day, we notice the effects of our meddling most clearly when it's hot, readily believing that we are to blame as yet another temperature record is broken. It may not be very logical, but just as I now feel disconcerted by hot weather, I can't help but draw a little comfort from the coldest days. They seem to offer hope that nature has retained at least some of its power and all is not yet lost. We are heating the planet to a dangerous extent, but when everything is white, and the ground is rock-solid

---

* McKibben, B. (1990) *The End of Nature*. Viking, London.

underfoot, I can, more easily, push that thought to the back of my mind.

A few years ago, when we lived in the Fens, the overnight temperature on a bitter February night fell to a record −14°C. I let the dog out into the garden first thing and stood motionless in the porch for a few minutes in my dressing gown, soaking up the raw power of air on skin – a power that was all the more impressive for the stillness and silence that accompanied it.

I've come to realise that my most firmly engrained memories of wild landscapes involve severe weather and snow. I've always been drawn to cold places, including the far north of Scandinavia, and the high mountains of Europe and further afield. We visited Poland a few years ago specifically to enjoy a cold, snowy eastern European winter. Arriving on 22 January, timed, we hoped, for the very depths of winter, we were distraught as the plane came into land to see no trace of snow. From the airport, we drove east to the ancient forest of Białowieża on the border with Belarus, passing through a dispiriting landscape of muted greens and browns.

A few days later, the snow arrived. We were told it was the first significant fall of the winter, just a few inches at first, but followed by unrelenting extreme cold and further snow on most days. It was so cold that at night we would hear rifle shots through the forest as the tree sap froze and expanded, cracking the wood itself. We would pause each evening at the hotel entrance, en route between bar and bedroom, to listen out for it. I have fond memories of the wildlife we saw: Wild Boar in the forest, a glimpse of Bison through the trees, Waxwings in the gardens and Sea Eagles circling over frozen lakes. But it's the weather and its effects on the landscape that stand out most strongly when I think back to that trip.

These are all things to ponder in the dark, dying days of the year in late December. A brand-new year is just a few days away. From here on, light levels will gradually increase as the nights shorten and the sun rises higher in the sky each day. The birds will respond to increasing day-length and begin to sing, some of them before the month is out. With luck, the landscape will be transformed by a blanket of snow for at least a few days in the months ahead. And, if not, there will surely be some 'ice days' to enjoy. The light on clear, frosty days will be spectacular, with a low sun to highlight the texture of the countryside to full effect. The cold, if fully embraced, will have an invigorating appeal, making time spent outside a joy, and coming back indoors an equal pleasure.

Added to all this, the regenerative power of spring will be there waiting, just around the corner; there will be a few more signs each week – from the increasing birdsong to the earliest flowers pushing up through the soil – that it is on its way. As with all of life's great pleasures, it is only possible to enjoy spring to the full because it is a reacquaintance after a period of absence. Even if you love spring and summer, and really do hate winter, it still serves its purpose. Winter (and wintering) has much to offer. But if you are unconvinced, it can at least be celebrated for the things it makes us wait for.

INDEX

Also available from Pelagic Publishing

The Hen Harrier's Year, by Ian Carter and
Dan Powell (coming summer 2022)

Low-Carbon Birding, edited by Javier Caletrío (coming summer 2022)

*Wildlife Photography Fieldcraft: How to Find and Photograph
UK Wildlife*, by Susan Young (coming summer 2022)

*Treated Like Animals: Improving the Lives of the Creatures
We Own, Eat and Use*, by Alick Simmons (coming autumn 2022)

Ancient Woods, Trees and Forests, edited by Alper H. Çolak,
Simay Kırca and Ian D. Rotherham (coming autumn 2022)

Essex Rock: Geology Beneath the Landscape,
by Ian Mercer and Ros Mercer

Bat Calls of Britain and Europe, edited by Jon Russ

Pollinators and Pollination, by Jeff Ollerton

The Wryneck, by Gerard Gorman

Wild Mull: A Natural History of the Island and its People,
by Stephen Littlewood and Martin Jones

Challenges in Estuarine and Coastal Science,
edited by John Humphreys and Sally Little

A Natural History of Insects in 100 Limericks,
by Richard A. Jones and Calvin Ure-Jones

Writing Effective Ecological Reports, by Mike Dean

*A Field Guide to Harlequins and Other Common
Ladybirds of Britain and Ireland*, by Helen Boyce

pelagicpublishing.com